Basics of Rational-Emotive Behavior Therapy

Milenko Vlajkov

Basics of Rational-Emotive Behavior Therapy

Acquiring Therapy Skills Step by Step

Springer

Milenko Vlajkov
Institut für kognitives Managment
Stuttgart
Baden-Württemberg
Germany

ISBN 978-3-032-19447-3 ISBN 978-3-032-19448-0 (eBook)
https://doi.org/10.1007/978-3-032-19448-0

This Springer imprint is published by the registered company Springer Nature Switzerland AG
The registered company address is: Gewerbestrasse 11, 6330 Cham, Switzerland

Acknowledgments

Writing this book has been a journey spanning over the past 30 years. During this time, many people helped shape my ideas about the cognitive approach in psychotherapy, counseling, and coaching. All of them deserve my gratitude, though there isn't enough space to express my deepest respect.

First, I am genuinely grateful to all my patients who trusted me, followed my recommendations after completing regular therapy, and reported leading improved, more fulfilling lives afterward.

My wife, Simona Vlajkov, deserves countless thanks for editing many chapters and discussing ideas I was unsure about regarding clarity, usefulness, and scientific support. She also spent many days and nights reading the final manuscript, insisting on the reader's perspective, whereas I claimed that I had been the measure of all things, "existing, that they are, and not existing, that they are not."

For all technical support, communication with potential publishers, and especially for reminding me to keep working on this project even when I couldn't see a light at the end of the tunnel, I am deeply thankful to Miss Katharina Schmid. She also supported me in collaboration with the publisher.

To my friend Erwin Schütz, I am grateful for his unwavering support. He never lost faith in my work and stood by me through many challenging rounds of writing and rewriting chapters.

Finally, I thank my publisher for the support in preparing the manuscript for the scientific and professional community.

About the Author

Milenko Vlajkov holds a degree in psychology and a master's in work, industrial, and organizational psychology from the University of Belgrade. He began his career as head of the HRM department at a large company in Novi Sad. Four years later, he moved to the Novi Sad City Psychiatric Clinic, where he worked as a clinical psychologist and psychotherapist for eleven years. In 1987, after completing his habilitation, he was appointed a university professor of work, industrial, and organizational psychology. There, he led the department of the same name until he fled to Germany in 1991.

He completed specialist training in Cognitive Behavioral Therapy in Oxford and specialist training in Rational Emotive Behavioral Therapy (REBT) in New York at the Albert Ellis Institute. There, he also became a member of the "International training center and policy review committee" appointed.

Milenko Vlajkov has lived and worked in Stuttgart since 1991. There, he founded the Institute for Cognitive Management as an "associated training center" of the Albert Ellis Institute in New York. To date, he has trained numerous psychotherapists in rational-emotive behavioral therapy and has never stopped actively practicing psychotherapy himself. The results of his psychotherapeutic experience are presented in this book.

Contents

List of Figures

List of Tables

List of Abbreviations

Abbreviation	Meaning
ABC Model	Activating Event – Belief – Consequence Model
A	Activating Event (the external or internal trigger for emotional responses)
B	Belief (the cognitive evaluation or interpretation of an event)
C	Consequence (the emotional and behavioral outcome of a belief)
APA	American Psychological Association
CBT	Cognitive Behavioral Therapy
DSM	Diagnostic and Statistical Manual of Mental Disorders
EQ	Emotional Quotient (emotional intelligence)
GAD	Generalized Anxiety Disorder
GP	General Practitioner
HFT	High Frustration Tolerance
ICD	International Classification of Diseases
IQ	Intelligence Quotient
LFT	Low Frustration Tolerance
NFT	No Frustration Tolerance
OCD	Obsessive–Compulsive Disorder
OST	One-Session Treatment
PR	Public Relations
PTSD	Post-Traumatic Stress Disorder
REBT	Rational-Emotive Behavior Therapy
USA	Unconditional Self Acceptance
WHO	World Health Organization

Chapter 1
Introduction

This book primarily aims to enhance the efficiency of psychotherapists in their practice. Additionally, the book has proven helpful for patients as a tool for bibliotherapy. Several manuals on Rational-Emotive Behavioral Therapy (REBT) have been written. Anyone holding the book in their hands rightly wonders why they should read this book, in addition to the books written by the founder of REBT, Albert Ellis. The book is neither more comprehensive, detailed, nor philosophically more profound than other REBT manuals. So why should this book be read anyway?

The book presents a clear structure for the therapeutic process. It enables the therapist to know at every moment of the therapeutic process how to steer "the ship" (the patient) out of a troubled ocean (emotional instability) into a safe harbor (emotional stability).

The book is stripped of all unnecessary explanations and thus represents the essence of a pragmatically oriented and practice-based therapeutic approach. The term "essence" refers not only to how psychotherapy should be practiced appropriately but also to what mistakes a therapist should avoid during a therapeutic session.

The book enables readers to acquire the basic knowledge of REBT and master the techniques that will help them thoroughly assist their clients in a very short time.

In this context, "thorough" means solving the problems that give rise to psychopathology and not just treating the symptoms caused by these problems. Therefore, the approach advocated in this book is based on identifying the causes of the disorder and eliminating them without linking them to the causes of other emotional disorders. In this way, a problem can be solved thoroughly. The expression "in the shortest possible time" refers to increased psychotherapeutic efficiency following the client's capacities. The efficiency of REBT lies in it requiring a significantly smaller number of therapeutic sessions compared to other therapeutic approaches. The expression "following the client's capacities" means that the therapist considers factors such as the client's age, mental abilities, and emotional state. The therapeutic process is compelling enough to achieve the desired therapeutic effect. This

M. Vlajkov, *Basics of Rational-Emotive Behavior Therapy*,
https://doi.org/10.1007/978-3-032-19448-0_1

means that the therapeutic result does not depend on the therapist as an individual, but instead on the therapeutic method and the therapist's skill in applying it.

In non-diREBTive psychotherapeutic counseling (according to Rogers), the basic means of therapeutic change are the therapist's empathy (the "warmth") and the client's acceptance of the therapist. Thus, this heavily depends on the therapist as a person. In contrast, REBT is a method by means of which the client is brought to an insight into the causes of his emotional disorders and motivated to solve his own problems. This is sufficient to achieve therapeutic change. That's why Albert Ellis, the founder of REBT, also insists, among others, on bibliotherapy (Albert Ellis, 2019). Hundreds of patients have successfully addressed their serious emotional issues by reading his books.

The manifestations of the problems are usually referred to as symptoms of the disorders, while the disorder itself is referred to as a syndrome in various classifications of mental illness (American Psychiatric Association [APA], 2013; World Health Organization [WHO], 1992, 2019). Since a syndrome is a collection of symptoms, the above classifications concern only a terminological change, not the designation of problems at two levels: the manifestation level and the level of origin. The manifestation of the problems is the collection of symptoms, collectively known as a syndrome. The origin of these problems is the cause of emotional disturbance, from which the procedure for solving emotional problems is derived.

For example, panic disorder is a syndrome upon which this disorder was named in the ICD-11. This syndrome consists of various symptoms that determine how the disorder is diagnosed. The symptoms are the manifestation of the disorder. The cause or origin of the disorder is a hidden thinking pattern. The therapist's task is to uncover this thinking pattern, examine it, and replace it with another one that works better for the patient.

Furthermore, this book presents the basic requirements that a trained therapist should consider if they want to open their therapeutic practice. This part of the book could also be helpful for all other professions in which the reader would like to become self-employed as a counselor or therapist.

The book's third and most crucial part relates to the chronological structure and components of the therapeutic process. In this way, those who wish to practice counseling or therapeutic work based on REBT are provided with the appropriate tools. They can not only help their clients solve their acute problems but also enable them to solve their own emotional and practical problems in the future.

This achieves the first goal of REBT: the therapist provides their clients with the knowledge and techniques to help themselves. Most therapists in other therapeutic orientations can plan their long-term financial income based on the therapies they are already providing, as they know how many of those therapies will continue in the following year. For example, a psychoanalytically oriented therapist knows that to complete a therapeutic process successfully, he will spend between 5 and 15 years with a client. If he has 20 clients who attend therapy twice weekly, the therapist's capacities are almost entirely exhausted. This means he can wait for the next year with peace of mind, regardless of whether new patients come.

Compared to such therapists, an REBT therapist or counselor is in a very thankless position, as the patient's current fundamental emotional problem is often solved in the first, albeit somewhat longer, session (e.g. specific phobias). Other emotional disorders (depression or various forms of anxiety) can be overcome within four to a maximum of 20 sessions. Patients with personality disorders are an exception, for whom it is necessary to schedule monthly so-called control sessions over a more extended period (every 1–3 months). Consequently, an REBT therapist or counselor could only plan their financial income if they had enough patients with personality disorders to care for. However, this would be very unpleasant for him because he would be constantly confronted with his failures. Patients with personality disorders are often resistant to treatment. The cognitive-behavioral therapeutic approach is one of the rare approaches that achieves lasting success, also with this pathology.

In his book "Managing People is Like Herding Cats," American author Warren Bennis (1999) describes the cognitive approach in career counseling and claims that managers often suffer from a personality disorder and require long-term counseling. The therapist can only hope his satisfied patients will recommend him to their friends, acquaintances, and relatives. However, this will only happen if the patient goes home after each session, not only satisfied but also enthusiastic. The therapist can respond to the question: "How do you manage to inspire your patients?" in several ways:

1. Use humor as an essential component of REBT as a therapeutic tool as early as possible because humor is the salt in the REBT soup. For example, the therapist cites humorous examples from everyday life that make the therapist and the client laugh.
2. The therapist should guide the patient to surprising insights so that he can recognize how his dysfunctional thought patterns are disturbing him.
3. Instructive stories from different traditions (Christianity, Hinduism, Buddhism, Zen, Sufism, etc.) can inspire the patient. This can help them deepen their understanding of the basic postulates of REBT and develop a willingness to learn and practice this new way of thinking. The patient is advised to share this content with others by actively using his knowledge and engaging in proselytizing, thereby indiREBTly recommending his therapist.

It is also crucial that the patient not only gains therapeutic insights during a session but also recognizes their value. This, in turn, leads to a gratifying sense of achievement that motivates the patient to continue therapy until they feel capable of solving their future problems independently.

Because emotional problems often permeate all areas of the patient's life, extending the patient's insights to all aspects of the patient's life is frequently necessary. The following metaphor illustrates this process: A person with a festering wound comes to the doctor. He is examined and treated. If his doctor does not clean the wound thoroughly, contamination can persist deep in the tissue, leading to renewed suppuration. Only after the cause of the wound's inflammation has been removed can the organism heal itself. Every emotional problem can be seen as a "mental festering" that spreads to different areas of life. Only the therapist who can use the therapeutic procedure—like a sharp surgical knife—is able to help the patient.

The insights brought psychoanalysis worldwide fame and enabled psychoanalysts to keep their patients convinced that they would be helped by these insights alone. This explains the relative ineffectiveness of the psychoanalytic approach.[1] The analytically oriented therapist usually leaves it to his patients to complete the therapeutic work—to apply the insights to everyday life and to make the newly acquired way of thinking a habit. Compared to REBT, the analytically oriented approach is more *indiREBT* and *passive*, whereas the REBT therapist or counselor proceeds in a *diREBTive* and *active manner* (Dominic Julien, Kieron O Connor: Comparative treatment Efficacy of Cognitive-Behavior Therapy and Short-Term dynamic Psychotherapy in High-Quality Studies: A Systematic Review and Effect Size Approach, *Journal of Psychology and Clinical Psychiatry*, 2016).

The following example illustrates the difference between the two therapeutic approaches mentioned above. During the diagnostic interview, a patient states that she has been undergoing psychoanalytic treatment for 5 years. When the therapist asked if this treatment had helped her, she replied, "Yes, it has helped me a lot." The REBT therapist then asked her why she had consulted him. She said, "Because I was getting worse and worse over the years." When confronted with the contradictory nature of her statements, she said that she had always felt comfortable with the psychoanalyst, except that this feeling of well-being had never been transferred to her everyday life. Another prerequisite for successful therapeutic work is the acquisition of masterful therapeutic skills. If the therapist can also playfully apply these skills, they will have the same effect on their patients as a magician has on his audience. The patient marvels at this effect as if it were a miracle. Just as the audience wants to see through a magic trick, the patient leaves the therapeutic session wishing to understand this magical therapeutic effect.

If the patient begins to apply the insights they have gained to solve their emotional problems independently, the REBT therapist has achieved the agreed-upon goal. He then initiated a process of change that encouraged the patient to follow this path to the end. For patients to recommend their therapist to others, the therapist must successfully convey the philosophy of REBT to their patients and clients so that they accept and represent it as their own philosophy. This philosophy is based on:

- Increasing frustration tolerance.
- The renunciation of the global rating of oneself and that of other people.
- Replacing absolutistic demands with flexible wishes and
- Increasing one's own flexibility by unconditionally accepting oneself, others, and life circumstances.

The strategic approach to therapy is explained at the end of this book. If the patient has several emotional problems, the therapist should address them one at a time, based on the patient's priorities. The treatment strategy differs for a depressed

[1] Cognitive therapy is structured and often short-term, lasting a few weeks. It is goal-oriented, focusing on specific issues such as anxiety, depression, burnout, and phobias. It focuses on identifying and altering dysfunctional thinking patterns into functional ones. It is present-focused, helping clients develop coping strategies for current problems. Cognitive therapy is evidence-based and empirically supported. Psychoanalysis is generally a long-term process that can take years, focusing on deep-seated psychological problems and exploring the unconscious mind. It explores past experiences and supposed unconscious drives, but often lacks empirical support.

patient compared to a patient with a generalized anxiety disorder or a patient with a specific phobia. Manifest behavioral disorders, such as obsessive-compulsive disorder, require a different strategic approach than addiction to psychotropic substances, and so forth. When considering the outcome of psychotherapy, the strategy often plays a decisive role, especially in REBT. It is found that the therapist begins resolving the patient's problems without having conducted a detailed diagnostic examination of the causes.

The more accurately the diagnostic examination is conducted at the beginning of therapy, the more reliably the therapist can predict the treatment's course. This book primarily aims to enable REBT trainees to develop and improve their therapeutic skills. It is also designed for professionals who have already completed specialized training in REBT or CBT. Additionally, the book is also intended for those who wish to strengthen their therapeutic skills and broaden their therapeutic competence through a well-structured therapeutic process. Academics, especially those with emotional problems or blockades, can use this book for bibliotherapy. Reading alone is usually not enough to overcome their problems. Professional help is often indispensable even for these people. This book is also recommended for professionals who regularly work with others (social pedagogues, doctors, dentists, teachers, educators, personal trainers, coaches, and those involved in counseling).

The more accurately the therapeutic model considers the patient's reality, the less time and energy the therapist needs to achieve a vital therapeutic effect. In contrast, other therapeutic models construct reality based on the model itself. This creates an imagined reality for the patient that does not closely correspond to the patient's actual reality. At any rate, this may explain why almost any therapy can be successful, provided it is given enough time for the patient to learn and internalize the therapeutic model. This also explains why REBT tends to be more effective than other therapeutic approaches. The model on which REBT is based is very straightforward and largely in line with the patient's reality.

Of course, REBT can be criticized for being too diREBT. This objection can be countered with a counter-question: Can something that leads diREBTly to insight into the cause of the emotional problem be too diREBTive, or is it only diREBT?

In his book "Reason and Emotion in Psychotherapy" (1994), Albert Ellis explained that the diREBT route to his clients' insights helped most patients more quickly than a psychotherapeutic approach he had previously practiced.

A second point of criticism is often found in the literature, namely that REBT is a superficial form of therapy that does not deal with the unconscious, underlying causes of the disorder. REBT therapists refute this criticism by assuming that irrational thinking patterns are responsible for dysfunctional emotions. Thinking errors arise from these thinking patterns, which in turn generate emotional problems, but the patient is not yet aware of this at the beginning of therapy. The fact that the patient is not yet aware of the true causes of their problems at the beginning of treatment does not indicate that they lie in the "unconscious"; it only means that they do not yet know anything about these causes.

The third and most significant objection to REBT is that it is ineffective in bringing about more profound personality changes. This objection is paradoxical because, on the one hand, some critics of REBT criticize that it influences and changes the patient's reality far too much through its diREBTive and active nature. On the other hand, REBT is said not to lead to any significant change in the client's personality. Above all, REBT enables the patient to overcome their fears and replace them with courage, to free themselves from depression, and to develop a healthy optimism. REBT can help a person who is emotionally unstable and behaves impulsively to become emotionally stable and more able to cope with life's difficulties. In this sense, such a change, should it lead to a personality change, is desirable for every patient.

Part 1
Theory of Rational-Emotive-Behavioral Therapy

Chapter 2
Theoretical Foundations of REBT

What is REBT?

Rational-Emotive Behavioral Therapy (REBT) is a structured therapeutic approach that helps clients solve their emotional problems and overcome their blockades on their own. To this aim, REBT provides the therapist with numerous cognitive, emotive, behavioral, and complex procedures and techniques.

For example, suppose a patient complains about typical age-related problems, such as losing interest and fear of the future. In that case, the therapist will first help them understand the causes of their loss of interest and then use cognitive corREBTions to help them adopt an optimistic attitude toward reality. The therapist will then support the patient in finding meaningful content to bring them back to life. In the first phase of therapy, cognitive techniques are used mainly; in the second phase, a combination of cognitive and emotive techniques is used, and in the third phase, behavioral procedures are added, which only make sense if the client has practiced cognitive methods until they have become automatic.

Practicing cognitive techniques implies that the patient acquires the ability to think "corREBTly," meaning rationally, in a problematic situation, and act appropriately. Acting appropriately means assessing a situation objectively, especially when it is critical. The patient should act efficiently to achieve appropriate results given the circumstances, thereby minimizing any potential harm.

This can be seen in the following example. A client became depressed after losing his leading position in a company. He blamed himself for not doing enough to keep his job. He then visited his GP, who only prescribed him tranquillizers. With an REBT therapist, he learned to accept what had happened unconditionally. This enabled him to stop his tormenting thoughts. Once he had internalized the new mindset of unconditional acceptance, he freed himself from his depression. Together with his therapist, he developed a plan to find a new job. After just a short time, he was appointed managing diREBTor at another company, where he

M. Vlajkov, *Basics of Rational-Emotive Behavior Therapy*,
https://doi.org/10.1007/978-3-032-19448-0_2

continued applying the new mindset until it became automatic, enabling him to resolve any unpleasantness constructively. His career was subsequently even more successful than before.

The therapeutic changes are initiated within a session and are only implemented and consolidated in the client's everyday life. Within therapy, clients learn how to solve their emotional and practical problems. The therapist should take particular care to avoid promising to solve the client's problems, but to focus on providing them with the techniques and knowledge to solve the problems on their own. The client will then be able to apply these techniques whenever problems arise. The therapist also explains to the client how to use the knowledge and skills they have acquired in everyday life in the long run. The primary purpose of the therapy sessions is to create a basis for therapeutic change in the client. Ultimately, the client is responsible for making the change happen themselves.

For this reason, therapeutic homework assignments are an indispensable part of REBT. To transfer the knowledge learned in therapy into everyday life, the client must consistently practice the assigned homework. The therapist designs these individually and adapts them to the client's needs. The client should treat them like medication to be taken daily.

The ABC Model of Emotions

The ABC model is the cornerstone of REBT.

The letter **A** denotes the so-called activating event. An activating event can be practically anything: an external stimulus, a physical sensation, a feeling, or a thought. If, because of one or more thoughts ("I have to do my tax return. I don't have time to do it, and the documents are scattered all over the house."), we think of something that follows ("And that's terrible because I won't be able to get everything done on time."), which causes an unhealthy feeling to arise (e.g., the fear of not receiving a tax refund from the tax office), then the first perceived thought of filing the tax return before deadline is described as an activating event, and the second thought ("it's terrible"), which is related to the first, as an irrational belief that needs to be examined and corREBTed.

The letter **B** (Beliefs) denotes precisely this belief, that is, the evaluation of the activating event. If an evaluation corresponds to the activating event, that is, rational, it leads to an emotional reaction that is adequate to the activating event. If the evaluation does not correspond to the activating event, it will result in an inadequate emotional reaction to the activating event. Consequently, evaluations can be logical, helpful, reality-based, and feasible (i.e., rational) or illogical, harmful, not reality-based, and not viable (irrational).

The letter **C** (Consequence) denotes the emotional and behavioral consequence that results from the client's thinking (**B**) concerning a specific situation (**A**). The consequences of thinking can be helpful to or blocking for the person concerned. If they are blocking, this manifests itself in the following ways:

Table 2.1 Unhealthy and healthy unpleasant feelings

Unhealthy feelings	Healthy feelings
Anger, rage, hatred	Irritability, frustration, dissatisfaction, disappointment
Depression, hopelessness, despondency	Sadness, grief, regret
Fear, panic, anxiety	Concern, caution, courage
Feeling insulted, offended, or hurt	Disappointment
Bad conscience, feelings of guilt	Remorse ("I'm sorry"), regret
Shame	Disappointment, regret
"Black" envy	"White" envy
Pathological jealousy	Non-pathological jealousy

1. The person suffers.
2. The person is mentally blocked, meaning they cannot think clearly.
3. The person behaves inadequately in a situation.
4. The person shows acute symptoms of stress (palpitations, sweating, a feeling of powerlessness, stomach cramps, etc.).
5. The person suffers from psychosomatic disorders (drop in immunity, hormonal disorders, functional digestive, and respiratory disorders).
6. The person has motivational problems (the motivation to carry out an upcoming activity is either excessive or insufficient).

A healthy, beneficial feeling arises for the person when the client appropriately evaluates the activating event. This is expressed by the following:

1. The person does not suffer even though they feel uncomfortable.
2. The person can think clearly and orient themselves well in each situation.
3. The person's behavior is functional, that is, goal oriented. The person endeavors to change the situation as quickly as possible for their benefit and, if this is not possible, accepts it as it is.
4. Acute physical symptoms are only present to the extent necessary to mobilize resources. There is no exaggerated reaction of the autonomic nervous system.
5. The right attitude eliminates psychosomatic disorders, promotes health, and increases immunity.
6. The motivation is optimally adapted to the circumstances.

Healthy and Unhealthy Feelings

In the cognitive therapy framework, there is no clear boundary between what Albert Ellis, the founder of REBT, described as healthy and unhealthy feelings. His colleagues, Aaron Beck (Beck, 1979), David Clark (Clark & Beck, 2011), and other therapists working in the cognitive therapy tradition believe that the transition between healthy and unhealthy feelings is gradual. This distinction is crucial because it determines the nature of the therapeutic approach. Cognitive therapy aims to reduce the intensity of unpleasant feelings, regardless of whether they are healthy or unhealthy. Albert Ellis makes a strict classification regarding feelings (see Table 2.1): He distinguishes between healthy feelings, which can be both pleasant and unpleasant, and unhealthy feelings, which, in his opinion, only include unpleasant feelings. However, the author of this book also considers some pleasant feelings to be unhealthy, noting that they can have a blocking effect on the individual[1] (see Table 2.2).

The rest of the text contains a table with unpleasant, unhealthy, and unpleasant healthy feelings.

Albert Ellis names three criteria that can be used to distinguish unhealthy feelings:

1. The person suffers.
2. The person is mentally blocked.
3. The person does not behave appropriately in the situation.

The following classification of healthy and unhealthy unpleasant feelings builds upon the theoretical distinction originally proposed by Albert Ellis (1994) but has been reformulated and expanded for contemporary REBT practice.

However, obviously, there are several other diagnostically relevant criteria for unhealthy feelings in addition to Ellis's criteria. As mentioned in the previous chapter, these are:

1. Acute physical symptoms,
2. Psychosomatic disorders, and
3. Motivational problems.

In this context, it is important to emphasize that everyone decides for themselves whether they describe a feeling as unpleasant and unhealthy or as unpleasant but healthy. Further on in the text, the position of Stoic philosophers will be explained in more detail, as they believed that it is not the things themselves that are the cause

Table 2.2 The difference between unhealthy and healthy unpleasant feelings

Unhealthy feelings	Healthy feelings
Mental suffering (psychological pain)	No suffering, only discomfort
Mental blockade	Mental flexibility
Self-defeating behavior	Helpful behavior
Inadequate motivation (over- or under-motivated)	Optimum motivation and activity level
Physical (stress) symptoms	Situation-appropriate physical activity Condition
Long-term psychosomatic problems (e.g. headaches, migraines, digestive problems, high blood pressure …)	Promotion of health

[1] The author replaced "negative feelings" and "positive feelings" with "unpleasant feelings" and "pleasant feelings," because "negative" and "positive "are evaluations whereas feelings are experiences

of our suffering, but the way we think about them. The fundamental task of any therapy session based on REBT is to out unhealthy feelings and replace them with the corresponding healthy feelings, which may still be unpleasant, depending on the situation. An unhealthy feeling can be debunked by identifying the thought responsible for it. In REBT, it is assumed that a change in thinking brings about a change in feeling. This assumption has proved corREBT in most clinical cases, although there are a certain number of cases where the change in mindset did not result in the desired emotional change. One reason for this may be that the person concerned does not believe sufficiently in the truthfulness of the rational statement. Another reason may be the patient's low frustration tolerance. If the patient considers even the unpleasant healthy emotion extremely unpleasant and demands that it not be there, he or she will continue to suffer.

Pleasant feelings can also be categorized as healthy or unhealthy. Healthy, enjoyable feelings inspire *joy* and optimism, whereas unhealthy pleasant feelings lead to illusions and a lack of motivation to address the task at hand. Unhealthy, pleasurable feelings often lead to problems like procrastination. For instance, someone overwhelmed by intense infatuation may be unwilling to study despite having an upcoming exam. Instead, they focus on things that boost their infatuation. When someone is caught up in excitement, they have a strong need to experience it fully, and if overwhelmed, they are reluctant to return to everyday life or complete necessary tasks. A person excited about a project may dedicate themselves to it out of enthusiasm, neglecting other responsibilities. In all these cases, we see emotional blockades, even though the person finds them extremely pleasurable.

1. Infatuation
2. Delight
3. Enthusiasm

It could be argued that any feeling that turns into ecstasy has a blocking effect because it prevents the person from completing critical daily tasks. Sometimes, however, it is desirable to experience something ecstatically. If someone taking part in a sports competition is in a euphoric state, they will be able to surpass themselves and achieve better results. So far, we can only partially explain how ecstatic feelings come about. We know, for example, that they arise when a person achieves a desired goal after long-term efforts or when they accomplish something they perceive as an extraordinary success. Unfortunately, such feelings do not last very long, although they are experienced as very intense and pleasant.

There is another feeling that is pleasant but has a blocking effect. This is the feeling of bliss. It would be difficult to find a person who does not want to feel blissful. Still, it is also clear that a person in this emotional state is unable and unwilling to engage in serious and responsible activities. In other words, the state of bliss is a pleasant emotional blockade.

The third type of blockade is indifference or a neutral relation to the content we are dealing with. In this respect, relaxation techniques are not a desirable form of therapeutic intervention because they can lead the practitioner to develop a certain indifference to reality.

The Role of Beliefs and Thought Patterns

Irrational beliefs give rise to so-called derivatives, which are diREBTly responsible for emotional disorders. Irrational beliefs can be recognized by four essential characteristics:

1. They are illogical or inconsequent statements (this will be discussed in more detail elsewhere).
2. They are not supported with the facts.
3. They cannot be implemented.
4. They are harmful to those who think them.

Albert Ellis (Reason and Emotion in Psychotherapy, 1994) collected irrational statements from his clients until 1978. Once he had collected 287 different forms of irrational beliefs, he analyzed their content and classified them into four categories of irrational thinking patterns:

1. **Catastrophizing:** When a client believes that reality is more than 100% bad and expresses this by stating that something is terrible or horrible. Catastrophizing as a mindset can be applied to three domains:

    a. On yourself, by describing the result as terrible after a failure.
    b. To other people, if, for example, someone is late despite promising to arrive on time: "It's terrible that they've kept me waiting so long."
    c. On circumstances: "It's cruel that it's raining right now when I've planned a barbecue with my friends, although it hasn't rained all summer!"

2. **Low frustration tolerance:** In technical jargon, the abbreviation "LFT" (low frustration tolerance) has become commonplace. It is expressed in a statement, "I can't stand it!"—a circumstance the client is firmly convinced of, even though they have often been bearing what they say they can't stand for years.
3. **Global rating:** Statements with which the client describes current circumstances, other people, and themselves with expressions that refer to a permanent state rather than a single event. A global rating is, for example, when a woman who has said something negative about another is labeled a "blabbermouth" or when someone who, out of ignorance, claims something that does not correspond with reality is labeled a liar. The term "blabbermouth" or "liar" implies the conviction that this person was, is, and will remain like this. Another example of a global rating is when we label ourselves as lazy, unreliable, immature, irresponsible, and so on. These statements indicate that we are convinced that we were like this in the past, are like this now, and will remain like this forever. It can, therefore, be summarized that a noun or an adjective expresses a global rating. The solution for such statements is to replace them with a description of concrete situations or to express them with a verb. It is advisable to answer the question of what the person did, when, and how they did it because, in this way, we limit ourselves to the event in question and do not judge the person. In this way, we create a feeling that is

adequate to the concrete situation, namely, a negative attitude towards what happened. However, since generalizations are avoided, we do not begin to hate this person.

4. **Absolutistic demands:** According to Albert Ellis, this thought pattern underlies all emotional disorders. An absolutistic demand can relate to life circumstances (my life circumstances must be perfect for me), to other people (every person I have anything to do with must behave perfectly towards me), or to the person themselves ("I must be perfect"). The main aim of REBT is for the client to recognize and examine their irrational beliefs and replace them with thought patterns that are more logical, congruent with reality, and beneficial for the client. Since the client often firmly believes in his irrational beliefs and the conclusions he draws from them, the therapist's task is to make the new, logical, and reality-based thinking patterns more credible to the client than the old, habitual ones. This can only happen if the therapist mutually examines the client's previous beliefs, challenges them, and helps the client formulate alternative beliefs that are more consistent with reality. The therapist then has the task of reinforcing and consolidating the client's newly acquired way of thinking, leading to immediate improvement.

The therapist's next step is to use procedures to continually reinforce those thinking patterns that are useful for the client, even if they are not to the client's liking. In this way, the client can automatically react to the same unpleasant circumstances with thinking that is appropriate, logical, useful, and practicable in the situation.

Absolutistic demands are usually the cause of emotional suffering. In REBT, they are referred to as rigid thinking patterns. Such thinking patterns are contrasted with a flexible way of thinking, which includes desires, preferences, and wishes. This type of flexible thinking is known as rational.

Analogous to the irrational thinking patterns mentioned above, the following rational thinking patterns can be defined:

1. An appropriate assessment of unfavorable events: Instead of thinking something is terrible or horrible, an unpleasant or adverse event is seen or described as "bad."
2. A high frustration tolerance, also named HFT (high frustration tolerance). Albert Ellis explored the low threshold for tolerance of unpleasant events and identified two forms in which it manifests. One form, which is also the most common cause of anxiety, panic attacks, and specific phobias, he referred to as NFT (no frustration tolerance); the second one, which is familiar to most people, he denoted as LFT (low frustration tolerance). Suppose we are exposed to an unpleasant situation. In that case, it is usually about a stimulus we perceive as physically or psychologically unpleasant, or the anticipation of physical discomfort, which may also result in emotional pain. This gives rise to two possibilities:

   a. To evaluate the physical discomfort as unbearable or
   b. To evaluate it as unpleasant but bearable.

If we think it is unbearable, we will treat it as a huge threat, like a danger we must escape at all costs. However, if we find it unpleasant but bearable, we will expose ourselves to it, tolerate it, and achieve the desired goal, assuming it is beneficial for us.

When the author of this book was in New York in 1989, he lived in the Bronx, in an outer borough. Once, he went to the bank to transfer money. The outside temperature was 40 °C. St. Arthur Avenue was empty, except for a fly on the street. The fly tried to stick to the sweat on his face, and he wanted to keep it off. When he entered the bank, a bank employee in a starched white shirt, tie, and black pants welcomed him. The room was air-conditioned in an American way—probably not more than 16 °C. He greeted them (the fly and the author) with a smile. When he saw the author all sweaty, he explained in detail why air conditioning was mankind's most significant achievement and that he could not imagine surviving these temperatures without it. It was evident that he felt his frustration tolerance was insufficient and would probably suffer badly if he had to survive without air conditioning. Such a frustration tolerance would undoubtedly be labeled NFT by Albert Ellis and would probably be replaced in the therapeutic session first by LFT and then by HFT (high frustration tolerance). As a homework assignment, Ellis would probably tell him to stop turning on his home air conditioning and ask if he occasionally goes to the sauna. If the bank employee answers that he likes going to the sauna and can withstand temperatures of 90 °C, Ellis would conclude that he would then probably also be able to tolerate the temperature of (only) 40 °C until evening comes. The air cools down on its own. He would also mention that generations of people used to live—and survived—without air conditioning and that even today, only a tiny percentage of humanity has the privilege of air conditioning, even though the majority live in tropical or subtropical regions.

3. Unconditional self-acceptance, unconditional acceptance of other people, and the life circumstances—instead of condemning and globally evaluating reality when unpleasant, it is merely described as unpleasant. Ideally, we can name precisely what we do not like. In this way, we realize that reality is neither good nor bad but only consists of good and bad events or occurrences.
4. A flexible way of thinking about what could happen—instead of thinking in terms of "either-or," the future is seen as a field in which several alternatives exist. Most future events are on a scale between two extremes, with only a few at either end of the scale.

Types of Absolutistic Demands

Albert Ellis has found that all irrational thinking patterns can be traced back to three fundamental demands. These categories and their corresponding emotional consequences are summarized as follows:

1. Demands on oneself—this pattern can be expressed as the following: "I must be good at everything I'm doing, and if I don't achieve perfect results to get recognition from others, I'll be less of a person, and that would be terrible!" This way of thinking usually generates anxiety, depression, shame, and guilt.
2. Demands on others—an example of this pattern would be: "You must treat me fairly so that I feel pleasant and happy! If you don't behave so, it would be horrible because I can't stand it when people treat me that way!" The second pattern relating to absolutistic demands is global rating: "If you don't treat me the way I consider proper, you are a bastard who deserves to be punished!" Such irrational beliefs, as a rule, cause anger, rage, hatred, and aggressive behavior, and can also be expressed through passive–aggressive and destructive behavior.
3. Demands on the world and life circumstances are usually expressed as follows: "My life circumstances must not deviate significantly from what I want, or else it would be horrible and unbearable for me! The only remaining thing in that case is to pity myself!"Such demands can cause depression, self-pity, and problems with self-discipline, such as avoidance behavior and procrastination of important tasks.

Chapter 3
Thinking Errors

The term "thinking errors" comes from cognitive therapy and is known in English as *cognitive distortions* (the literal translation would be distorted thinking). Cognitive distortions refer to formulations that patients use to describe their own reality. They are seen as the diREBT cause of emotional problems. The difference between irrational beliefs and thinking errors is that irrational beliefs are thinking patterns, while thinking errors are only manifestations of these beliefs, that is, their derivatives.

Here are some examples that explain the relationship between irrational beliefs and thinking errors: If someone demands of themselves that they must be perfect at every moment, then this is an irrational belief—an absolutistic demand that they pose on themselves. For example, the following thinking error could be derived from this demand: "If I'm not perfect, then I'm faulty goods!"

Another example is expressing an irrational belief through catastrophizing. If someone thinks, "It's terrible that I've had a headache for three days," and then concludes, "It will never go away!" the second statement is a thinking error because it doesn't correspond with reality.

The author's classification of thinking errors in this chapter is based on a systematization made by David Burns in his book "Feeling Good" (Burns, 1999). Those interested in the details are recommended to read this work. However, Burns makes no distinction between irrational beliefs and thinking errors, that is, their derivatives. Instead, he places irrational beliefs in the category of thinking errors. Despite this, it is helpful to learn the numerous examples described in this book, as they help one better understand thinking errors and apply this knowledge to one's own life.

However, the author's experience to date has shown that this distinction is important because it increases therapeutic efficiency. Suppose only the thinking error is corREBTed in therapy without identifying the irrational belief at its core. In that case, the patient is only enabled to recognize and corREBT the thinking error he has made so far, but not to detect the irrational belief underlying this thinking error. Mistakes will continue to happen in this case, regardless of the number

M. Vlajkov, *Basics of Rational-Emotive Behavior Therapy*,
https://doi.org/10.1007/978-3-032-19448-0_3

of therapeutic sessions, because the core irrational belief from which they originate has not been eliminated. The author calls this phenomenon "lawn mowing" vs. "uprooting."

This can also be illustrated by the following comparison: If a thinking error represents the physical symptoms of a disease, the irrational belief is like the cause of that disease. Treating emotional disorders by corREBTing thinking errors is equivalent to using aspirin to reduce the increased body temperature caused by, for example, dental neuritis.

Here is another example from the author's practice: A company manager came to therapy and stated that he felt listless, lethargic, and depressed, which indicates a depressive syndrome. When asked what was going through his mind when he felt like this, he replied that he was thinking he couldn't get anything done, nobody respected him, and that he was the most unsuccessful in his job. After corREBTing these three thinking errors related to his reality, which will be explained in detail later, he was ready to replace them with the "right," that is, realistic way of thinking. It turned out that he had, in fact, succeeded in many things and that the statement that he had not succeeded in anything was unrealistic. At the heart of this thinking error is the absolutistic demand that he must succeed in everything he tackles, even things he has never done before! The irrational belief that underlies this thinking error is: "I have to be perfect to earn the respect of others." When the company manager realized that reality didn't correspond with his idea of himself, this irrational belief gave rise to a thinking error. Because, even if he had been the most unsuccessful of all the people he knew, he wouldn't have felt depressed unless he continued to demand of himself that he be a perfect manager.

The real cause of his emotional problems was, therefore, not his thinking errors but the irrational beliefs from which these errors arose. Thinking errors are a part of everyday life and are often used to emphasize or better describe a situation. Because of their great literary value, they are an integral part of human communication. Problems arise only when the thinking error leads to an emotional overreaction to the corresponding subject matter. If the error in reasoning has arisen from an irrational thinking pattern, it simultaneously reinforces this thinking pattern. Thinking errors cannot be eliminated from language because they are a linguistic instrument of humor, sarcasm, irony, cynicism, and social criticism. In addition, they can be used to articulate certain content even more convincingly, whereby they are, at the same time, also the royal road to form and consolidate irrational thinking patterns.

It is advisable to get familiar with the thinking errors described in this book and to become aware of them continuously for a few weeks by reading the newspaper, watching television, and listening carefully to the people you talk to daily. In this way, anyone can develop immunity to the so-called "mental contagion." This is possible if you increase your frustration tolerance by exposing yourself to stimuli that are perceived as unpleasant.

Temporal and Spatial Generalization

Temporal Generalization

Errors related to temporal generalization involve terms such as "always" or "never." Examples of this are: "I (always) make mistakes all the time" or "I never feel happy." It is evident that the first statement does not correspond to reality because no human has constantly made mistakes in the past, is currently making mistakes, and will continue to do so in the future.

Suppose we want to make a statement with a time reference. In that case, it is advisable to replace the expressions "always/all the time" and "never" with the expressions "occasionally/most of the time." In this way, the sentence "Sometimes I make mistakes" corresponds more closely to reality. The same applies to the statement, "I'm never lucky." If you replace the word "never" with "now and then," you get the statement "now, and then I'm not lucky," which is true for most people.

However, simply corREBTing thinking errors is not enough because, as mentioned, these are based on irrational beliefs. These beliefs are not changed by merely corREBTing the thinking errors ("lawn mowing") but by addressing the absolutistic demand through a preferential attitude (meaning "uprooting"). Thus, the irrational belief "I must not make mistakes!" or "I must be happy!" forms the core of time generalization. The rational alternative to this is "I very much want to be happy all the time, but as I'm not, I don't have to be." In the case of the irrational thought pattern "I mustn't make mistakes!," the rational alternative is "It would be desirable never to make mistakes, but since I can't prevent this from happening sometimes, they can happen!"

In cognitive therapy, a therapeutic process exists that recognizes and corREBTs thinking errors, which corresponds to symptom treatment in a medical model. On the other hand, recognizing and corREBTing irrational thinking patterns corresponds to causal therapy in the medical model. A particular form of cognitive therapy is known as "schema therapy" (therapy with cognitive schemas, whose core assumption is that cognitive errors and pitfalls are the consequence of hidden cognitive schemata).

Spatial Generalization

This thinking error is expressed by using terms such as "all," "everything," "nothing," "everybody," and "nobody." If the thinking error relates to an object, the following example would be suitable: Someone goes shopping and tries to find an appropriate piece of clothing. After being unsuccessful in checking out a few stores, the person concludes: "Everything is so tasteless! No matter where I look, I can't find anything that fits!" This is a case of spatial generalization because the whole is considered tasteless and inadequate based on the experience in some stores. The corREBTion of this thinking error consists of merely describing the concrete situation. This would then read as follows: "Nothing here appealed to me; everything I saw here seemed tasteless to me." In this way, the person avoids believing that the whole reality is distasteful and inadequate.

The second variant of spatial generalization refers to people: if someone says, for example, "Nobody likes me" or "Everyone just wants to take advantage of me," they overlook the fact that some people genuinely like them and mean well. Obviously, the phrases "nobody likes me" and "everyone just wants to take advantage of me" do not correspond to reality. These thinking errors can be corREBTed on two levels: the first is to replace the expressions "all" or "none" with "some," as in: "Some people don't like me, and some want to take advantage of me." In this context, it's about the first corREBTion level, as the patient's statements are aligned with reality.

Statements that are entirely in line with reality would describe the specific situation, for example, "Person X doesn't like me" or "Person Y tried to take advantage of me**."** The emotional reaction to such a statement would relate only to this situation and not carry over. However, in this case, it is only a symptom treatment because, at the core of this thought, there is the absolutistic demand: "People should like me," and "They shouldn't take advantage of me." A rational alternative to the conviction "People must like me" is: "It would be nice if people liked me, but since it happens time and again that they dislike me, they don't have to like me!" The rational thought behind the absolutistic demand: "People must not take advantage of me" is: "I wish that other people would not take advantage of me, but if I can't prevent it and it has already happened that they had taken advantage of me, then I didn't have to prevent it either." The sole corREBTion of the thinking error and a description of reality do not lead to an improvement in the therapeutic sense. Still, the shift from irrational to rational thinking patterns is bringing about essential and long-lasting therapeutic changes.

Jumping to Conclusions

This thinking error consists of two parts. The first is the description of the circumstances; the second is a statement apparently based on them. An example is when someone wakes up in the morning with a slight tension in their head and thinks: "Oh my God, if I feel like this in the morning, what will my day be like?." This question assumes the day will be terrible and the headache unbearable. Behind this thinking error is, on the one hand, the unspoken demand that one should feel refreshed and pain-free in the morning after sleep, and, on the other, the assumption that if one already feels this way in the morning, their condition will only worsen throughout the day.

The corREBTion to this thinking error is as follows: "It is true that I have a headache. My condition could stay like this, get worse, or get better. Based on my previous experience, I know that every headache I've had has gone away after a while, so this one will most likely go away, too." If we ask a person how they feel when they think like this, they will probably answer: "Relieved and unburdened," whereas with the first-mentioned thought—the abrupt conclusion—they would probably answer: "Burdened, with even more pressure in their head." Jumping to conclusion is based on an irrational belief in the form of:

1. Absolutistic demand, which is a fertile ground for developing thinking errors, or
2. Catastrophizing and
3. Low frustration tolerance

So, this irrational belief takes the form of an absolutistic demand: "After sleep, I should feel good and have no pain at all!" The rational alternative to this is: "It would be nice if I always felt pain-free and well after waking up. Since it wasn't always like that, it doesn't always have to be like that!" Actual therapeutic change in the client only occurs when he recognizes this irrational demand and replaces it with the rational, flexible way of thinking mentioned above.

Thinking errors can often serve as a signpost to unmask underlying irrational beliefs. In therapy, the therapist first tries to identify the irrational thinking. If the client does not get insight into the relationship between the irrational belief and the emotional state, then it should be looked for thinking errors. By corREBTing them, we show the client that it is possible to change their emotional state by altering their way of thinking.

Mental Filter (Selective Attention)

A mental filter thinking error reflects the patient's present cognitive and emotional state. "Cognitive state" refers to an attitude towards a person or content. For example, if someone has a negative attitude towards women, they will look for things in every female that confirm their attitude because their attention is selective. The typical example of how the emotional state affects selective attention arises in the case of a generalized anxiety disorder. In this case, the person only focuses on the dangers in a particular situation, thereby reinforcing their anxiety.

For this reason, they will also attribute an impairing effect to neutral content. For example, a person will perceive driving a car as an endangering situation due to their generalized anxiety disorder (constant fear), even though it is an everyday and neutral situation and activity. For example, when somebody is overwhelmed with anger, they will focus on the contents that will justify and ultimately intensify anger. Or they must be 100% sure that all electrical household appliances are switched off, focusing their attention exclusively on them and checking several times in succession whether they are indeed switched off.

In all these examples, the emotional state is the filter that only allows certain information into consciousness, in fact the information, which is congruent with the current emotional state.

Mental filters not only generate selective attention but also alter perception, causing even neutral content to be labeled as impairing or unpleasant. An example of this is when a depressed person cannot be happy about the lovely and sunny weather but instead thinks about what harmful effects the sun's rays could have on their skin. Similarly, a person gripped by anger thinks they see irony in the smiles of their friends.

Such clients can be helped to eliminate their symptoms by pointing out the presence of a mental filter and teaching them to adjust their perception of reality. In this way, people who are only looking for danger due to a generalized anxiety disorder can be offered a broader spectrum of information about reality. A person overwhelmed by anger should be sensitized to the components of reality that are unrelated to their rage. In this way, anger can be mitigated. Similarly, you can find neutral content for depressed people and thus reduce their depression. A fundamental therapeutic change results from discovering and corREBTing the core irrational beliefs from which the mental filter originates.

Disqualifying the Positive

Situations in which you are expected to behave modestly, or you even assume that something like this is expected of you, often lead to the thinking error known as "disqualifying the positive." For example, if someone is complimented with, "Your presentation was very good," many people respond out of false modesty with: "Yes, **but** I wasn't that well prepared!" or "Still, I made two mistakes!" instead of simply saying thank you and accepting the praise. It is also typical when the person who was told that the sweater they are wearing looks very good on them replies: "**But** it's not really fashionable anymore; I bought it three years ago." This thinking error arises if the irrational belief "I mustn't show any weakness!" is at its core. (The "weakness" in this context would be believing that the three-year-old sweater is still good.) Such clients show a symptomatic improvement when they are sensitized to this category of thinking errors and learn to accept compliments and thank others for them. The next step is to recommend that whenever they recognize a thought unrelated to acceptance or gratitude, they are advised to abandon it and stop repeating it in their minds immediately. The essential therapeutic change occurs only after replacing the irrational belief that underlies this thinking error with a rational belief. This rational belief could be, for example, "I wish I would not express any weaknesses, but since I have them, I don't always have to hide them, and they may come out!." In this way, the person can communicate unburdened and express joy when they receive a compliment, even if others judge this expression of joy as a weakness.

Personification

Personification as a thinking error consists of the conviction that when I suffer in an interaction with others, it's because of the others, and vice versa: when the others suffer in a certain context with me, then I am responsible for their suffering. For example, suppose someone is told to format the reports they are responsible for better next time, and they then think this person only wants to humiliate them and demonstrate their power. In that case, they are making a mistake known as "personification." The feelings that usually arise from personification are mainly hurt and anger, and corREBTing the underlying thinking alleviates those feelings. The irrational belief that others must behave perfectly towards the person who holds this demand is at the core of this thinking error. The fundamental therapeutic change—liberation from the feeling of hurt—lies in replacing the irrational belief with a rational one: "It would be preferable for people to treat me fairly, but if they don't, then they don't have to!" Since most patients are not receptive to a fundamental therapeutic change (recognizing the irrational belief and replacing it with the rational one), it is advisable first to corREBT the thinking errors to achieve symptomatic improvement and only then, using the "inference chaining" procedure (explained in the chapter "The inference chaining"), to gain a more profound therapeutic change.

Emotional Reasoning

This thinking error manifests as the belief that the ultimate proof of facts and reality comes from a gut feeling, or intuition, that arises in a specific situation. Instead of interpreting one's thinking as the source of feeling, the feeling is argued to be proof of the corREBTness of one's own thinking. Examples of this type of emotional reasoning are: "I have a feeling in my gut she doesn't like me," "Intuitively, I know he won't come," and "My gut tells me she's wrong." In all three examples, it's all about assumptions from which the feelings originate. For instance, if a child hasn't put their toys away after playing, their mother might "freak out" and shout at them, if she believes her gut feeling tells her the child deliberately left a mess. Suppose you point out to the mother that her rage stems from her mistaken belief that her own feelings are the ultimate proof that her child *deliberately* provoked her rage by not putting away their toys. Of course, most patients in this situation would say they wouldn't have been enraged if the toys had been put away. So here we have the case of both thinking errors: absolutistic demand on a child (He should put away his toys!) and, on top, emotional thinking regarding his behavior (My "gut" is telling me that he did that *deliberately*!) This can be communicated to the client by addressing their irrational beliefs on a philosophical level, specifically by clarifying that reality is not always pleasant or easy, and that we have **a choice about how to respond**. So, she is faced with the option of either remaining in the realm of healthy feelings or causing self-induced emotional pain.

Only when the client expresses a desire to feel healthy can it be explained to them that their thoughts diREBTly determine how they will feel—in other words, whether they react to a situation with healthy or unhealthy feelings. You can then return to the problem with which you began the therapeutic intervention: it is not the mess in the room that caused the rage or anger, but the belief (in one's own feelings) that the child *deliberately* left the mess!

Early-career therapists are advised to use such situations as a hypothetical-deductive model, as this is the preferred way to develop the patient's capacity for insight. Should the patient have reservations about the cognitive model of emotional suffering, it is advisable to remind them of the critical distinction between healthy and unhealthy feelings whenever they address a situation with specific emotional problems. In the case of emotional reasoning, it's about believing one's own gut feeling, which is actually the result of an assumption.

So, emotional thinking can be corREBTed by making the patient aware that their feelings result from an assumption. This awareness leads them to relativize the objectivity of their statement, thus producing a therapeutic effect that diminishes the intensity of their inadequate emotional reaction.

Mind Reading

The thinking error known as mind reading is expressed in statements such as: "She only said that to hurt me," "She wants to provoke me with these words," "He keeps quiet for fear of upsetting me," "She averts her eyes because she doesn't like me," "He is not answering my letters because he wants to avoid me," and so on. All these statements share the common element of attributing thoughts, feelings, and behavior to one person, leading to the second person's corresponding emotional reaction to the first. This thinking error can be corREBTed by asking, "Can I really know what the other person is thinking, or can I only make assumptions?" If you find it a guess, it would be good to see a few more possible interpretations that could explain the other person's words or behavior. In other words, what else could be the reason for the statement or behavior in question?

Well, the person might have just answered a question without thinking about how it would affect you. They may have assumed that you would like their statement; they may have just been trying to be funny, or they may have been frightened and, out of fear, phrased their statement in such a way that it sounded like they were trying to offend you. Silence, for example, does not necessarily mean that someone is afraid—usually, it's simply because the person has nothing to say.

If someone averts their gaze, it may be because there is something more interesting to see, since, according to the laws of the Gestalt theory of perception, something new and moving spontaneously attracts attention, in contrast to objects that are already known or that do not move. If someone does not answer a letter, it may be because they have not received it or because answering it is not a high priority.

If they consider a letter necessary, they may want to answer it but need more time. They may need more time now due to other obligations, and so on.

What-If Thinking

The concept of "what-if thinking" suggests that someone who thinks this way is constantly looking for threatening or catastrophic contents. If a caring mother asks herself, "What if my child doesn't notice that the traffic light is red and just runs into the street?" and she already imagines it under the wheels of a car, then despair will take over. If a businessman starts to imagine what will happen if he loses his main customer, who accounts for 80% of his total annual turnover, panic will set in. In the worst-case scenario, this could lead to him closing his company or even committing suicide instead of objectively assessing whether it is at all likely that he will lose the customer and whether he could survive without him.

This thinking error can be corREBTed by helping the client become aware of opportunities rather than worrying. For if a person's attention is only occupied by worries, he will not notice the opportunities that arise time and again throughout his life but will instead slip into depression or—as it is known in the working world—suffer burnout syndrome (a modern term for everything associated with chronic stress). The corREBTion involves systematically focusing attention on opportunities for several hours each day. Whenever the person notices that the thought "what if" comes up, they should replace it with the question: "Has this day brought me any chance for change in the diREBTion of improvement?"

Believe Your PR Agent

Usually, a person's friends, parents, and relatives have a better opinion of that person than other people. If you ask the former for their opinion of the person's actions, they will often give positive feedback. As a result, over time, the person starts believing that he or she is more capable than is the case, possibly developing an arrogant attitude towards reality based on overconfidence. This can lead to what is commonly known as "pride comes before a fall" or, to put it even better: "The higher the fly, the deeper the fall." To corREBT the mistake of overestimating oneself, it is advisable to cultivate modesty instead of arrogance, avoid global rating, and only evaluate specific events and results.

On the same token, if someone believes that their reference persons who are putting them down or belittling them are right, they will feel bad about themselves, thinking they are inferior or not capable enough, and so on, and thus be mentally and emotionally blocked, with low self-confidence and low or no motivation to achieve personal goals.

Chapter 4
The Three Insights

REBT has its roots in the philosophy of the Stoics of ancient Greece and Rome, with its leading representatives being Seneca (4–69 CE), Epictetus (50–135 CE), and Marcus Aurelius (121–180 CE). All three came from different social classes and lived at various times. Marcus Aurelius was a Roman emperor, Seneca a philosopher, and Epictetus the slave of a slave. And yet, all three came to the same conclusion.

The causes of human suffering are not things in themselves but the way people think about them. This is the first of three fundamental insights on which REBT is based. It determines the strategy of this form of therapy.

Albert Ellis defined three types of insight. He referred to the first insight as cognitive insight, the second as emotional insight, and the third as behavioral insight.

The First Insight

The reason why people suffer does not rest in the things themselves but in the way people judge them. Recognizing this is enough to bring about a therapeutic change in those who suffer. However, this implies that people know:

1. What did they think about what they perceived?
2. How did they feel while they were thinking it?
3. How can they verify what they believe?
4. What can they think better instead of the thought that has caused them an emotional problem?
5. How can they consolidate the new thought that is objective, truthful, logical, and consistent with the facts?
6. How can they connect the new thought to their reality so that it automatically comes to mind in a critical situation?

M. Vlajkov, *Basics of Rational-Emotive Behavior Therapy*,
https://doi.org/10.1007/978-3-032-19448-0_4

The points listed belong to the cognitive realization of the causes of one's emotional distress. Only when the patient recognizes how they are to think rationally does the process of their recovery begin. A sudden insight into the connections often accompanies this realization. However, the patient usually remains in doubt, and this prevents them from experiencing emotional insight. In most cases, doubters even claim that the solution to their problems cannot be that simple. The therapist must next free the client from their doubt. Ellis calls this process a dispute, or challenging irrational thinking and replacing it with rational thinking. However, rational thinking still lacks power at first, and it is only when the client begins to believe the new thoughts that emotional insight arises.

The Second Insight

A therapeutic change can be achieved when rational thoughts replace thoughts that cause emotional disturbances. At this point, it is important to note that rational thoughts need not be positive; they are simply thoughts that correspond to reality. If you only try to think positive thoughts, you will make a mistake known as "positive thinking." Using positive thinking is advisable only when a person is completely helpless in their circumstances and when these circumstances are extremely threatening. Positive thinking then generates hope and confidence that the dire circumstances will not last forever. In this way, the person concerned can bear their suffering better because they see it as temporary, even if the circumstances never improve.

However, there are also extreme and perverse forms of positive thinking. One of them is the belief that thoughts can influence material reality. Some proponents of positive thinking claim that if you think about getting sick, you will get sick, and this belief can lead to illness. In return, however, it would do to believe in your recovery for it to occur. Neither the first nor the second assertion has been confirmed experimentally. The opposite has been proven. For example, if someone thinks something is dangerous, this may motivate them to accept the danger, confront it, and tolerate the discomfort of the hazardous situation. However, if you think something is harmless, even though it is harmful, you may not be sufficiently motivated to confront it. This often produces lethargy and flabbiness.

The assertion that believing in recovery through the "power of thought" is enough to get well has also proven to be false. Such thoughts have little healing power; they merely encourage the sufferer to endure the illness. This often prevents the person concerned from taking the necessary steps towards recovery promptly, such as having a medical examination and taking the appropriate medication.

Albert Ellis introduced emotional insight into the theory of cognitive behavioral therapy, stating that a qualitative change in feeling occurs after the client has accepted rational thought as believable.

The resulting feeling differs from the feeling caused by positive thinking. With positive thinking, you can put yourself in a pleasant state, even in difficult situations. A healthy feeling is the result of cognitive insight, which need not be pleasant. If someone is confronted with unpleasantness, the healthy feeling is dissatisfaction. Positive thinkers would describe dissatisfaction as a negative feeling. But the very word "negative feeling" contains an evaluation. However, feelings cannot be negative; they can be pleasant or unpleasant. The prefix negative is used to describe an undesirable feeling. However, if a feeling is unpleasant and, at the same time, healthy and appropriate to the circumstances, then this feeling is conducive to the circumstances with which one should be able to cope efficiently. These unpleasant but healthy feelings mobilize physical and mental resources to the extent necessary to cope with the situation in the best possible way.

The Third Insight

Emotional disturbances do not last just half an hour or two days, nor are they only present when activating events occur. On the contrary, once a disorder develops, it can persist for months. The main types of emotional disturbances are anxiety, depression, and anger. They result from ongoing self-indoctrination through self-destructive thoughts. For the patient to permanently free themselves from suffering, practicing a new way of thinking is necessary until it becomes automatic. This explains why the therapeutic process in REBT involves several phases: the first phase leads to the first insight, the second to the second insight, and the third to the third insight. Finally, the fourth phase allows the patient to return to real life.

The third insight pertains to changes in behavior following the first and second insights. The second, emotional insight, leads to new, constructive actions in the same situation where a person, for example, previously engaged in avoidance behavior.

A highly relevant case demonstrates how behavioral insight can benefit the individual involved. The author once worked with a client who was afraid of flying. The client was a representative for a large pharmaceutical company responsible for all of Europe. His job involved frequent visits to clinics across the continent to present new medications and research findings from his company. Sometimes, he traveled over 1000 km a day in his own car. He met the author by chance through a friend and asked if his fear of flying could be overcome. His fear stemmed from a single irrational thought: "I can't bear to get on an airplane." It took less than a minute to test this thought. When asked if he would die if he boarded a plane, he replied, "No, I wouldn't die." At that moment, he recognized that the only proof against his fear was the possibility of death. He was visibly relieved. This shift in thinking alone provided an emotional insight. The client then rephrased the rational thought in his own words: "It would be tough to board the plane, but I would survive."

Then came the ultimate test: his first flight in an airplane. During the flight, he spoke to the therapist as if he were in his office, not on an airplane.

The client experienced all three insights in a single day and session, and this was reinforced until the fear transformed into a sense of courage.

Two weeks later, during another meeting, it became clear that the client had integrated his new behavior so thoroughly that he could no longer imagine not flying an airplane. He has been flying through the clouds around the world for 21 years now, and he finds it even enjoyable!

Chapter 5
Wishes and Demands

Albert Ellis has shown that people tend to transform their wishes and desires into absolutistic demands, especially when they consider these desires to be important. The fact that the transformation of wishes into demands happens quickly and often, has led Ellis to assume that this mechanism is biologically determined and has a specific adaptive value, being developed through evolution. So far, it has been shown that this tendency is strongly present in most people and that only a few people do not have it or can keep it under control. Based on this, Ellis concluded that his therapy is suitable for everyone and that it would be desirable to use a psycho-educational process to enable children to think "corREBTly," meaning rationally, to prevent the development of emotional disturbances.

Even if someone has been brought up very rationally and has grown up in optimal living conditions, they can acquire irrational thinking patterns and begin to suffer accordingly (through anxiety, anger, emotional instability, impulsivity, depression etc.). People tend to produce emotional disturbances through irrational thinking by turning their desires into demands. Fortunately, they can also recognize their irrational beliefs and turn them back into wishes, thereby freeing themselves from emotional disturbances. The fact that people are driven by both tendencies indicates that while REBT is not the only path to absolute mental health, it is a very reliable tool for overcoming emotional problems. We cannot stop the brain from producing thoughts because this is its primary activity. Still, we can recognize the thoughts that the brain produces and evaluate them as rational or irrational, or as beneficial or harmful. You can then replace harmful thoughts with useful ones or irrational ones with rational ones.

To show in detail how you can help yourself and your patients overcome emotional problems, the following section explains the standard procedure *for a psychotherapeutic session.*

M. Vlajkov, *Basics of Rational-Emotive Behavior Therapy*,
https://doi.org/10.1007/978-3-032-19448-0_5

Part 2
The Practice of Rational-Emotive and Cognitive Behavioral Therapy

Chapter 6
The Therapeutic Process

The Outline of an REBT Session

The standard scheme of a psychotherapeutic session based on the REBT method consists of the following steps:

1. Questioning about the problem.
2. Agreement on the problem being worked on in the session.
3. Looking for the specific emotional and behavioral problem (C) or activating event (A).
4. Checking for the presence of a secondary emotional problem (symptom stress).
5. Deciding which problem to solve first—primary or secondary emotional problem.
6. Defining the goal of the psychotherapeutic session—how the client would like to feel in the same situation, including possible corREBTion if the client chooses an unrealistic goal.
7. Explaining the link between (B) and (C)—the role of thinking/judgment in the emotional problem (usually by using an example).
8. Identifying a specific situation in which the emotional problem arises.
9. Searching for the irrational belief (B)—using the "inferencechaining" technique.
10. Establishing the BC connection regarding the current problem, which is being addressed in the therapeutic session.
11. Verifying (challenging) irrational beliefs through the logical, empirical, pragmatic, and deductive dispute.
12. Formulating rational alternatives.
13. Converting cognitive insight into emotional insight.
14. Converting emotional insight into behavioral insight.

M. Vlajkov, *Basics of Rational-Emotive Behavior Therapy*,
https://doi.org/10.1007/978-3-032-19448-0_6

15. Encouraging the therapeutic process by being sensitive to the statements "should," "must," and "ought to." Motivating the patient to recognize these words as a guide to irrational thinking patterns. The recommendation is that the patient also offer advice to others based on the knowledge he has acquired in therapy.
16. Homework (cognitive, emotive, behavioral, complex).

Chapter 7
Questioning About the Problem

The therapist begins the session by asking the client what problem they would like to solve. The client answers the question by describing one of the two aspects of the problem:

- He describes a practical problem. For example, the client says he must choose between two career options and is still indecisive about which one would be more beneficial.
- Or he might also describe an emotional problem. In the example above, the client says that he is afraid of making a wrong decision because he believes it must be made irrevocably.

Sometimes, clients answer questions about their problems by saying they have so many issues that they don't know which one to start with. Then, they describe in detail not only the current problem but also a large part of their life story, thinking they have to say everything they find problematic. To help the patient focus on the problem that brought them to therapy, it is advisable to guide them toward describing only current events and the related emotional states. If the client tends to ramble, asking them to define the problem in one or two sentences is also helpful. If this does not work and the patient continues to give detailed accounts of their life events, then it makes sense to ask them to express in one sentence what bothers them most and what they want to resolve in this session. This often occurs with patients who have already undergone other psychotherapeutic treatments. Patients treated by analytically oriented therapists find it particularly difficult to pinpoint their problem and be concise. If the patient lacks experience or knowledge of the cognitive-behavioral approach, the therapist should introduce the framework to establish a foundation for effective psychotherapy.

M. Vlajkov, *Basics of Rational-Emotive Behavior Therapy*,
https://doi.org/10.1007/978-3-032-19448-0_7

The Therapeutic Framework of Cognitive-Behavioral Therapy

Over the past few decades, humanistic and behavioral approaches have developed alongside the analytical approach. All these methods aim to address emotional problems effectively. However, they differ in the time required to resolve emotional problems. For the same issue, some therapies may take several years, while others need just a few weeks or one or two sessions.

Cognitive behavioral therapy (CBT) and REBT are forms of therapy that often require only a few sessions to solve a problem, sometimes even just one. Modern society demands that its members treat others' time with respect. For example, a business consultant who offers services to a particular company is expected to achieve the agreed results as quickly as possible. The cognitive-behavioral therapist and REBT therapist, respectively, think similarly: he will best approach them if he respects their patients' time and strives to achieve significant therapeutic change as quickly as possible. Following these, the rules between the therapist and the patient are also defined in this sense.

One rule is to focus the patient's attention on the fundamental problem or to diREBT it toward solving only one emotional problem within a session. The patient should be informed that a therapeutic session lasts a maximum of 50 minutes.

The description and identification of the emotional problem to be solved during this interval should take no more than 5 minutes, ensuring that both the patient and the therapist mutually commit to considering it. Therapy is structured into intervals of a set duration. The therapist respects this until the patient becomes familiar with the therapeutic process. Patients who understand the therapy's time frame become active collaborators in each session, which is why this therapy is considered active and diREBTive, especially regarding the therapist's role.

How Should the Question About the Problem Be Formulated?

Many therapists start by asking what problem the patient wants to work on today. Based on his 50 years of therapeutic experience working with individuals and companies, the author has concluded that the most efficient question is as follows:

What Is the Most Important Problem You Want to Solve in This Session?

This formulation focuses the patient's attention diREBTly on solving the problem. Other formulations include: *"What would you like to discuss with me today?" "What would you like to start with today?" "What problem would you like to solve today?"* or *"How are you?"* However, these formulations slow down the therapeutic process instead of facilitating and accelerating it.

The question *"What would you like to discuss with me today?"* activates patients' need to express themselves and share anything that is bothering them. However, it does not guide them towards a constructive search for a solution to the problem, which prolongs the treatment.

The question, *"What would you like to start with today?"* can lead the patient to want coffee or tea, a light chat about the weather, or perhaps a vacation. Most people put off unpleasant topics for later because they consider them private matters. People only talk about their private lives after they have developed a closer emotional connection with the therapist.

The question *"How are you?"* is not part of the therapeutic process, but it encourages the client to discuss the issues that interest them most. In most societies, the cultural stereotype is to answer "good" or "excellent." If people are "contaminated" with positive thinking, they will reply "good" or "excellent" even when they feel bad or miserable. They are convinced that their emotional state will deteriorate even more if they say something bad about it.

Some patients react negatively to the word "problem," especially those who have already experienced some form of systemic therapy, positive thinking, or so-called positive psychology (Seligman, 2004) and positive psychotherapy (Peseschkian, 2016). Positive thinkers and proponents of positive psychology and psychotherapy claim that the word "problem" alone could create problems. This view is particularly prevalent in the business world, where many managers and professionals believe that only solutions, not problems, should be discussed. This is why the word "problem" is used at the beginning of the therapy. You can only solve something if the subject that needs to be solved is named. So, you solve problems, not solutions; therefore, we can't just talk about solutions. Suppose some clients insist that using the word "problem" in the psychotherapeutic session is unnecessary. In that case, it is helpful to replace this term with the term "task," and if this also does not meet with a favorable response from the client because it reminds them of school and negative school experiences, then it is good to talk about the goals to be achieved. Suppose the therapist does not use the word "problem." In that case, he can formulate the question as follows: "What would you like to change in your life at this moment?" or "What would you like to achieve in the course of the therapeutic session?" or even more precisely "What is the most important thing you would like to change or achieve in the course of this therapeutic session?" Thus, the client's attention is focused on solving the most crucial problem and the therapist achieves a double effect:

1. The client usually selects the problem he can't solve on his own, that causes his suffering. As a result, he will be highly motivated to work on the solution.
2. The bigger the problem, the easier it is to solve. This statement contradicts the belief held by other therapeutic approaches that one should start by solving easy and simple problems. These therapists argue that it is vital to treat patients gently and then guide them step by step toward more severe and complex problems.

However, this unnecessarily prolongs the therapeutic process. Apropos, this is not the primary goal of therapy! The basis for the assertion that more severe problems are more accessible to solve is that when the therapist diREBTs the patient's attention to the most important problem, the patient is less likely to be distracted by "harmless emotional problems." In perceptual psychology, it is known that a person can only deal with an issue without digressing if they are emotionally committed to this activity. Focusing on the most important problem enables the therapist to identify the unhealthy feelings associated with it more clearly. In this way, therapeutic cooperation can be easily established and treatment goals formulated, resulting in a significant therapeutic effect from the very first session. Patients cannot recognize their most important emotional problem if they find themselves in one of the following situations:

3. Patients believe that they are responsible for solving their problems.
4. They believe that they have already solved the most important problem.

In this case, the therapist should ask, *"What is currently bothering you the most in your everyday life?"* Before this, however, it would be useful to explain to the patient that it is human to have problems. This would encourage the patient to talk about their problems.

The client can then focus on the issue that bothers them the most or that they want to resolve. If this approach doesn't work, the therapist might suggest common problems, such as procrastinating important tasks, avoidance behaviors, poor self-management, conflicts with others, or issues within the family or raising children. If these also don't produce results, it could indicate that the patient has no emotional problems or is unwilling to face them. This often happens when the patient doesn't seek therapy voluntarily but is pressured or coerced (for example, when spouses force their partners into treatment if they are alcoholics or drug addicts. Courts may also order re-socialization measures for individuals who have committed crimes for psychiatric reasons, like child pornography or other sexual offenses etc.).

These are just a few examples of resistance to therapy and a lack of willingness to cooperate with the therapist. If the therapist has the patient's data, collected through the diagnostic interview or psycho-diagnostic measuring instruments, then he understands the patient's core issues. As a result, he can plan and prepare the first therapeutic session and focus on addressing the most critical problem.

The next question is how the therapist can assess which of the listed problems to address first in the initial therapy session.

The therapist identifies the primary issue that most impairs the patient's ability to complete everyday tasks. For example, a person with generalized anxiety disorder might struggle to perform tasks effectively under heavy pressure. In this case, addressing the anxiety should take priority over other issues like depression, guilt, envy, or jealousy. If a roofer with generalized anxiety disorder suddenly develops a fear of heights, he will no longer be able to do his job. To help him most effectively, he should first work to overcome his fear of heights in therapy and then focus on managing the generalized anxiety disorder.

The question *"What do you suffer from most that you would like to get rid of?"* is only appropriate to a limited extent at the start of the therapeutic process.

The information gathered during the diagnostic interview is essential because it forms the basis for developing the therapeutic strategy. This emphasizes that the core idea of "cognitive management" involves overcoming efficiency blockades, with emotional blockades being the most significant among them (Vlajkov). In this book, the term "emotional efficiency blockades" is used because simply experiencing suffering or feeling distressed does not suffice to justify starting psychotherapy. In that case, their emotional state should hinder their ability to perform their daily activities. Only when this criterion is met does the therapist know what to focus on during the first session.

The next step to identify the problem that should be addressed in the first therapy session is to ask the client what they want to achieve, how they want to feel, or what results they hope to see. To help the client become more aware of the practical aspects of the problem, the therapist asks what knowledge and skills they would like to have gained by the end of the session to better handle challenging everyday situations.

If the client sets a specific goal for their first therapy session, they are asked what has prevented them from reaching it so far. This helps the therapist determine if they have identified the main problem.

The discussion about the problem should be completed with the fact that many theoretical approaches assume that patients already possess all the resources they need to solve their problems, and that therapy's goal is to activate them. That's like claiming that the client can play the piano with all 10 fingers without practicing just because he has 10 fingers.

If everyone had all the necessary resources, this would automatically mean they possess the required knowledge. Additionally, it would indicate that patients recognize that their emotional problems are not caused by objective life circumstances but by their thinking. As a result, they would also understand how to transform dysfunctional thought patterns into functional, rational ones.

Agreement on the Problem

Although the client usually offers one problem in response to the question, *"What is the biggest problem you would like to solve today?,"* they sometimes name several problems in succession. They cannot decide which of these they would like to solve first. The therapist and client agree on the most important problem to be resolved during the session. If the patient insists that all the problems he has named are equally important, he cannot choose one, as doing so would neglect the others. The therapist then has two options:

1. He suggests that the client start with one problem, solve it, and tackle the next one. He agrees with the patient on the sequence in which the problems should

be solved. In this case, the therapist considers the interdependence of emotional problems. If the therapist has discovered by means of a diagnostic tool that the patient suffers from a generalized anxiety disorder, is depressed, and occasionally has fits of anger with accompanying feelings of guilt, depression cannot be the first problem to be solved because depression is the consequence of several other emotional disorders (based on his many years of experience, the author asserts, that depression as a syndrome, in addition to the clinically relevant diagnosis, described in DSM 5, also consists of generalized anxiety, low impulse control, feelings of guilt, apathy, grievance, despair and occasional powerless outbursts of anger). It is clear from this that a necessary precondition for the successful application of the cognitive approach in psychotherapy is that the therapist can accurately diagnose their patients' or clients' mental disorders. Suppose the therapist does not possess this skill. In that case, he may choose problems that are not clinically relevant and those that are only symptomatic but have clinically relevant problems at their core.

2. If the patient cannot decide on any of the problems they have named, the therapist asks how they feel. This second approach assumes that the patient has an emotional problem or blockade that prevents them from choosing one of the problems mentioned. In REBT, this is referred to as a secondary emotional problem.

Suppose the client needs help in identifying the problem to be solved. In that case, the therapist should explain to them the role of emotional blockades and the distinction between emotional and practical problems from the perspective of the cognitive approach. At the Institute for Cognitive Management, Stuttgart, a specific psychoeducational procedure has been developed to help the client understand the cognitive model of the development of emotional disorders. The client is usually given the following explanation.

The Instruction *to* Distinguish *Between* Healthy and Unhealthy Feelings

> You probably understand what feelings are, but to ensure we're speaking the same language, I suggest you describe what you mean by a feeling. The client then typically responds, *"This is what I'm feeling."* The therapist then emphasizes the need for a precise description by reminding the client that it's possible to feel, for example, "heaviness" in the legs, palpitations, or other bodily sensations, but that these are not feelings; rather, they are physical sensations. He then asks the client, *"What are feelings? Which ones do you know? Please list some pleasant feelings!"* Then he asks the client to list some unpleasant feelings. He draws a two-column table: the left column for pleasant feelings, the right for unpleasant feelings. The right column is further divided into two sub-columns labeled *"healthy feelings"* and *"unhealthy feelings."*

The following example illustrates the instruction to distinguish between healthy and unhealthy feelings:

The client begins to list pleasant feelings, such as happiness, satisfaction, love, pleasure, delight, and so on. Regarding unpleasant feelings, he mentions dissatisfaction, grief, sadness, jealousy, envy, anger, hatred, and so on. Patients can usually list more unpleasant feelings than pleasant ones. After the therapist lists the patient's pleasant and unpleasant feelings, he asks the patient when and in what situations these feelings occur.

The client then replies that the good life situations are responsible for his pleasant feelings and the bad ones for his unpleasant feelings. If the client reports feeling good or enjoying himself, the therapist tells him that he does not need therapy because the client is already in a desirable emotional state.

If the client feels miserable, the therapist should determine whether the client is being blocked by the feeling dominating him or if it is helping him and enabling him to cope well with the critical situation. Only now does the client begin to understand that he should leave the choice of the initial problem to the therapist, even if he believes that all his issues are equally important and should be solved immediately. The therapist also explains to the client that some problems are interdependent. Therefore, addressing the problem chosen by the therapist can help resolve the client's other listed problems more quickly. For example, if someone suffers from a generalized anxiety disorder (it manifests as social anxiety in the presence of others, as agoraphobia, or as occasional anxiety attacks about unpleasant body symptoms, such as excessive sweating or flushing of the face), solving this problem will enable the client to cope with all concrete situations in which the generalized anxiety disorder manifests itself.

It often happens that patients believe they are on the verge of an imminent physical catastrophe, even though they are physically healthy. This fear of a physical disaster can be elegantly resolved by overcoming the generalized anxiety disorder first.

Chapter 8
Model of Development of Emotional Blockades

REBT is a therapeutic approach that helps patients solve their problems independently. The method promoted by the Institute for Cognitive Management Stuttgart complements and enhances REBT with tools that help patients address practical issues and improve their quality of life. As a result, clients are better able to set their own priorities, manage their time effectively, fulfill their obligations, and achieve greater success in life. Most patients experience emotional problems related to their practical issues, so they tend to resolve their practical problems almost automatically once they have overcome their emotional problems. That is why we refer to emotional problems as emotional efficiency blockades. The cognitive management approach assumes that nearly every client can learn various skills necessary for daily life. They can then use these skills to improve their own quality of life, especially communication skills and proper self-management.

To prevent clients from having false expectations about the solution to practical problems, the therapist should clearly explain the possibilities and limitations of REBT, while highlighting and clarifying the difference between emotional and practical problems. It is particularly important for a client to receive a brief explanation of the difference between unpleasant, healthy feelings and unpleasant, unhealthy feelings, as this is crucial for the success of the therapeutic process.

The following two problems may arise during a therapeutic session:

1. The client is troubled by their own unpleasant but healthy feelings and wants to free themselves from them. A good example is when the client feels tired after a sleepless night and interprets this as an unhealthy emotional state, even though this tiredness is a normal consequence of the sleepless night.
2. The client describes an unpleasant, unhealthy feeling using a term that is usually associated with an unpleasant, unhealthy feeling.

For example, a patient says that his girlfriend has promised not to be late in the future. However, she is late for the next meeting. When asked how he feels about this, he says he is disappointed, which leads the therapist to carefully examine his

M. Vlajkov, *Basics of Rational-Emotive Behavior Therapy*,
https://doi.org/10.1007/978-3-032-19448-0_8

Figure 8.1 Rebt-model of therapeutic change

feelings and identify it as a feeling of hurt. Possible reasons for mislabeling feelings include a patient's limited vocabulary and their difficulty in distinguishing feelings. The therapist should determine whether the term the client uses hides a healthy or unhealthy emotion. For example, the question "To what extent is the fact that you are disappointed a problem for you?" encourages the client to describe their emotional state more clearly. The therapist can then assess whether the client's feelings are functional or dysfunctional. Some clients respond when asked, *"What is the most important problem you would like to solve today?"* with: *"My children."* The question *"And how are your children your biggest problem?"* prompts the client to explain the problem in detail, for example, *"When I tell them to tidy their room, they only do it after I have shouted at them!"* The therapist's next step is to ask the client how he feels when he notices the children are not paying attention to him or following his instructions. From this point on, the therapist begins to clarify the client's problem using the ABC model of emotions.

Disobedient children are referred to in the ABC model as the activating event (**A**), and the client's feeling, in this case, anger, is the consequence (**C**). The ABC model explains the relationship between activating events, beliefs, and emotional consequences, as shown in Fig. 8.1. The therapist agrees with the client that anger is the first problem to be solved because anger is a dysfunctional emotion that prevents the client from controlling himself and, at the same time, blocks him (he shouts at the children and shows no willingness to negotiate with them). The goal of the therapy is to replace the client's anger with dissatisfaction, as dissatisfaction does not block him. Even if the patient feels dissatisfied, he can control his behavior and is motivated to solve the current problem as quickly as possible. If the patient has an unpleasant but healthy feeling, this feeling does not block his resources for solving the problem, while the emotional blockades negatively influence the client's behavior. Suppose the client has transformed his dysfunctional feeling into a functional feeling. In that case, he can think clearly and devise a meaningful strategy to make his children meet his expectations and clean up the room.

The most important therapy task at the start of the process is to help clients recognize their emotional problems as significant impediments and motivate themselves to address them. However, clients often blame practical issues for their suffering. They believe they can solve their problems through practical skills because they notice that they don't communicate well, struggle with daily life, and frequently have conflicts. This is why they prefer attending communication, time management, and conflict resolution seminars rather than workshops that help them recognize and overcome emotional blockades, thereby becoming more successful. The therapist should explain how feelings stem from specific thinking patterns and how these feelings can prevent them from completing everyday tasks. Most clients want to acquire skills to live better. However, many don't realize that improvement depends diREBTly on whether they are emotionally blocked. Some even resist addressing emotional blockades, claiming they are not blocked but only lack problem-solving skills. Therefore, raising awareness about emotional blockades as a primary cause of inefficiency is one of the therapist's most important tasks. If the client understands that thinking is the primary source of feelings, which in turn influence actions, they will realize that increasing behavioral efficiency requires changing their thinking.

Chapter 9
Frustration Tolerance

People with low frustration tolerance tend to improve their emotional state through behavior. Low frustration tolerance means that people with emotional problems become impatient and want to shake off what is bothering them immediately. An example is when someone fears a specific object or situation and flees from it or avoids it. People who get angry when confronted with an obstacle and try to get rid of it through aggressive behavior also show low frustration tolerance.

The solution to the two emotional problems lies in the insight that people mistakenly believe that they cannot bear the discomfort they are exposed to in the long term. This results in dysfunctional behavior that often does not produce the desired results. Only when these people have gained this insight can they review it and replace it with rational thinking. This enables them to tolerate the situation they are afraid of (cockroaches, spiders, bridges, cemeteries, etc.). Although people understand that they can solve their everyday problems more easily if they free themselves from the emotional blockages, they still believe that they can solve their everyday practical problems despite the emotional blockages. Only when they have confronted themselves a few times with their inability to control their behavior as desired do they realize that solving emotional problems is at the fore.

It would be preferable that a beginner in psychotherapy understand and accept that their clients come to therapy to suffer less. Most of the time, however, the client's emotional problem is not severe enough. Because of that, they are not sufficiently motivated to practice the cognitive skills necessary to solve emotional problems.

Clients with an emotional problem that they don't consider as very important quickly gain cognitive insight into its causes; however, they stop practicing the newly acquired way of thinking, which always leads to relapses. Ellis calls such patients with a weak emotional problem "fine, nice neurotics." These people are physically healthy, materially secure, and live in a family where the other family members tolerate their suffering and behavior and even show understanding.

M. Vlajkov, *Basics of Rational-Emotive Behavior Therapy*,
https://doi.org/10.1007/978-3-032-19448-0_9

However, they stand in their own way because they do not accept themselves unconditionally and have a low frustration tolerance. In fact, they seek someone to improve their mood as if by magic. In technical terms, these patients are called therapy resistant. They claim to suffer greatly and are the unhappiest people on earth, insisting that no one understands them. When the therapist examines their problem more closely, it becomes clear that it is not just a superficial practical problem but, more importantly, an emotional blockade that is not visible enough. This blockade is severe because, first, it prevents practical problems from being solved, and second, it causes suffering for the client. These clients find therapy even more arduous than continuing to tolerate their emotional problems. The first approach with such clients is to let them handle things on their own until they begin to suffer so intensely that they accept the therapeutic process and engage with it entirely. The second common approach is to accept the "fine, nice neurotics" as lifelong clients, with the therapist refraining from demanding cooperation for therapy to succeed. This practice likely stems from healthcare system rules: the therapist earns more if the client stays in treatment longer, rather than if they improve quickly. At the Institute for Cognitive Management, clients are encouraged to understand how emotional problems develop, adopt the new thinking model, practice it, and apply it to themselves whenever they notice emotional suffering.

The clients are encouraged to overcome the emotional problems first and only then deal with the practical problems and solve them constructively. To help them understand this process, we are explaining the following facts to them: overcoming emotional blockades enables the person to think more clearly, to feel less bad in challenging situations, and to act more calmly and more focused on goal attainment. If the client realizes that he is emotionally disturbed, he becomes aware of this and knows that the emotional disturbance is a consequence of his way of thinking. This way of thinking diREBTly prevents them from acting efficiently and solving the emotional problem constructively.

Emotional blockades manifest themselves not only through a limited ability to think and psychic pain but also through body tension, restlessness, excessive sweating, palpitations, dry mouth, and, now and then, the inability to prevent impulsive movements (tics, gestures, and body postures). Overcoming the emotional blockades frees the patient from the physical symptoms listed above, or it weakens them.

The alleviation of physical symptoms is particularly significant for clients who bring themselves to the next level of emotional disturbance via physical symptoms and develop, for example, a social phobia.

In the case of social phobia, it is advisable to assume that it is based on a generalized anxiety disorder, the root of which is at least one irrational thought pattern (catastrophizing) but manifests itself through a variety of thinking errors (derivatives). The deductions (derivatives) relate to evaluating situations that may threaten the client. For example: "If I start sweating, everyone will notice it and think I am ill or crazy, and I must prevent this at all costs! But if I fail, something terrible will happen; they will reject and laugh at me! That's why I should stay where I am instead of exposing myself to any social situation, because I could embarrass myself in any of these situations, or the others would laugh at me!" In this way, out of the generalized anxiety disorder, a social phobia is generated and, respectively, the need to avoid all social situations that are interpreted as dangerous.

Inexperienced therapists often overlook the fact that the likelihood of relapse is high in the clients described. Suppose the client with a social phobia based on a generalized anxiety disorder stops consistently exposing himself to social situations that are unpleasant for him. In that case, he will anticipate this unpleasantness, which will lead to his renewed avoidance behavior. Such a mistake will reduce the patient's efficiency in everyday life. The client addresses his therapist again with one of the following beliefs:

1. Either he believes that the therapist will help him again because he helped him last time, or
2. The client is overwhelmed by hopelessness because he does not think that the therapist will help him, as he did not help him last time either. Should the therapist have helped him, the client would not have relapsed.

The author advises therapists not to be misled by their clients' beliefs. Otherwise, they risk violating an important REBT guideline. That guideline suggests that the therapist confront the client with the worst possible outcome in a hypothetical situation to significantly improve the client's frustration tolerance. For example, even if a client has completely overcome social phobia, they might still feel uncomfortable around others. This feeling doesn't necessarily stop them from completing tasks. If a client always expects to appear confident, be in a good mood, and have everything under control, the therapist's job is to help the client let go of this false hope. The therapist should point out that the client doesn't necessarily need to feel good, even if they seem to have everything under control and can entertain others.

In that sense, REBT differs from other therapeutic approaches because it deals with the client's suffering unsparingly.

Some therapists make the same mistakes as friends do with each other. They comfort the client by telling him that everything will get better. Suppose the therapist allows himself to be influenced by the client's belief that he has helped him and will help him again this time. In that case, the therapist overlooks that the relapse has already reinforced the old thought pattern many times. For this reason, the therapist has a much more challenging task with the same client than he had at the beginning of the first therapy. It is recommended for the therapist to develop a clear strategy for the therapeutic approach. Additionally, the therapist should evaluate the client's progress and schedule follow-up sessions, even if the client claims not to need them. In cases like social phobia, initial control sessions are held every month and later every three months.

Suppose the therapist is guided by the client's belief that he was unsuccessful the first time. In that case, he should use the cognitive approach and compare the objective data with the client's beliefs. If the client has been able to expose himself to all social situations and succeed, there is evidence that the therapy was successful despite the current relapse.

There are two particular social situations where the client had better not be preoccupied with overcoming his emotional problems:

1. If the emotional blockade does not prevent the client from acting functionally and,
2. If his life is jeopardized, meaning exposed to a life-threatening danger.

In the second case, the client doesn't have time to overcome his fear because, in such situations, fear is functional and mobilizes all client resources to cope with danger successfully—either to defend himself or to flee (fight-or-flight). In all other cases, especially in harmless life situations where there is no real danger—only the one the client imagines—it is advisable to overcome the emotional blockade by changing the way of thinking.

Chapter 10
The Search for the Specific Emotional Problem (C) or After the Activating Event (A)

Once the problem has been defined and an agreement has been reached with the client about how to solve it, the therapist should explain the distinction between practical and emotional problems. If the client mentions a practical problem, the therapist then asks how the client feels in this challenging situation. The answer may indicate a healthy or unhealthy feeling.

Albert Ellis explained the difference between healthy and unhealthy feelings in many of his books. He argued that these are two distinct categories of feelings, not a continuum, because they are *qualitatively* different. In contrast, most other cognitive therapists, such as Judith Beck (J. Beck: Cognitive Therapy, Basics and Beyond, New York, 1995) or Raymond Di Giuseppe (in a lecture of internship 1995 at Albert Ellis Institute), claim that healthy and unhealthy feelings are part of a spectrum with a gradual transition. For this reason, some cognitive psychotherapists also consider dissatisfaction and disappointment to be clinically relevant problems, even though they are regarded as healthy feelings in REBT. In this text, Ellis's perspective is emphasized for the reasons mentioned above and serves as the foundation for therapy and counseling. Clients tend to accept the difference between healthy and unhealthy feelings more quickly than the idea of a smooth transition from unhealthy to healthy feelings. Therefore, they can apply this concept more effectively in their daily lives.

Albert Ellis distinguished between general REBT and *specific REBT.* General REBT is synonymous with cognitive-behavioral therapy (CBT), while specific REBT is a slightly different concept from CBT. Specific REBT is easier to apply, uses humor, and differentiates between thinking patterns and thinking errors (Dr. Albert Ellis: Reason and Emotion in Psychotherapy, New York, 1994).

REBT mainly focuses on emotional problems. When clients learn to manage their emotional problems, they often become better at handling practical problems as well. The therapist also assists some clients in resolving practical problems, especially when these solutions help speed up and support overcoming emotional barriers.

M. Vlajkov, *Basics of Rational-Emotive Behavior Therapy*,
https://doi.org/10.1007/978-3-032-19448-0_10

How Can Knowledge About Overcoming Emotional Blockades Be Applied to Solving Practical Problems?

A client who understands how emotional problems develop can better comprehend and more easily accept others who are emotionally disturbed, such as those who are anxious or angry. From the perspective of REBT, clients are advised to apply their newly learned way of thinking to those around them. This enables them to help friends and acquaintances become aware of their responsibility for their emotional problems. Only a few severe life events lead to profound life experiences. Usually, the client fears a self-created inconvenience, which they then see as a catastrophe that has already occurred.

Although a therapy session primarily targets emotional problems, the therapist also examines practical problems to understand the client's thought patterns better and gather enough information to question irrational beliefs. Therefore, it is necessary to focus on the activating events (**A**) and address them thoroughly.

Role and Types of Activating Events

Understanding the practical aspect of the problem allows the therapist to hypothesize about the client's thinking patterns that may underlie their emotional problems. It is easier for the client to remember what they thought during a problematic situation than to recall their thoughts in a specific emotional state. For instance, if the client mentions "fear of the elevator" as a problem and the therapist asks, "What do you think when you feel the fear of the elevator?" the client probably won't be able to remember the thoughts that caused their fear. However, if the therapist explicitly asks about the last time the client felt fear in the elevator, and the client recalls it. The question becomes: "What was going through your mind when you were overwhelmed by the fear of the elevator?"

The client will probably recall the thoughts that caused their anxiety. Suppose the client remembers this last concrete situation in which he was emotionally blocked. In that case, he can more easily understand that it was not the things themselves (i.e., the elevator) that were responsible for his emotional disturbance, but the way he thought about it: "The elevator is a dangerous place. Something bad is going to happen! I could get stuck, go crazy, or die! It would be terrible!" This leads to the following:

1. The client takes responsibility for their own emotional blockades because they understand that they have caused them.
2. He realizes that he is not helplessly at the mercy of his circumstances, but he can free himself from his emotional blockades, even if they persist.

There are different types of activating events. The easiest to identify are those related to the client's life circumstances and other people in their environment. Examples include the weather, when someone claims they became depressed because of bad weather; illnesses and other uncomfortable physical sensations; family, friends, work colleagues, and so on. It is more difficult to identify the real activating event if, for example, the client reports feeling anxious at a very attempt to recall a traumatic event. It would be premature to say that the actual activating event is a traumatic experience. A thorough review of the client's memory shows that it is not the event itself but the memory of this event that triggers specific thoughts, which then produce anxiety.

One Example:

T: *"When was the last time you had a panic attack?"*
K: *"When I thought about my stay in the hospital."*
T: *"What were you thinking?"*
K: *"That it would be horrible to experience it again."*
T: *"And if it happened again, what would that mean for you...?"*
K: *"That I will never free myself from the panic.... (starts crying)."*

Conclusion: The client does not have to go to the hospital to elicit his panic. His irrational thoughts are triggered solely by the memory of his last stay in the hospital, and from this, the concrete thought arises: *"It would be terrible if I had to go through the whole thing again ... "* This thought gives rise to fear, which then manifests itself through unpleasant physical sensations (heart pounding, sweating, cramped stomach, etc.) that he, in turn, interprets as a hint of the catastrophe to come. *"If I feel like this now, what would it be like should I have to go back to the hospital? Surely, it would be even worse than last time."* This thought intensifies the fear. The resulting discomfort is perceived as almost unbearable, which then results in a panic attack. The person wants to escape this intense fear and the associated physical sensations because they find them highly stressful. The panic triggers an innate reaction known as the fight-or-flight reflex. Trying to escape the fear and bodily sensations won't work, as one produces the fear and takes it everywhere in one's head.

Instructions for Identifying Activating Events

In the practice of REBT to date, various authors (i.e., Windy Dryden and Stevan L. Nielsen) have asserted that therapists with little clinical experience tend to ask questions irrelevant to therapeutic success (Dryden, 1995; Nielsen, 2001). Some therapists and counselors use language that is familiar to them but not understandable to the client. They encourage their clients to simultaneously look for several activating events related to an emotional problem.

To avoid the difficulties mentioned above, it is advisable for readers in specialized training in cognitive-behavioral therapies to note the following:

1. The therapeutic conversation should be managed so that the client does not add unnecessary details to their answers. Both the client and the therapist often lose focus on the main problem because they get caught up in peripheral details. They start discussing unimportant information and miss the session's main goal. To keep the client focused on what is relevant, the therapist should occasionally summarize what has happened during treatment. They should also point out the difference between relevant and irrelevant content. If the client does not allow the conversation to be guided this way, the therapist should politely interrupt their uncontrolled flow of speech by explaining that the information being provided is not helpful in solving the client's problem. Right after, the therapist should ask a question that rediREBTs the client to the central issue of the session. A helpful way to do this is:
2. The therapist should discourage the patient from using abstract terms or language that can be linked to universally accepted rules or principles or are considered individually as rules. Statements like "my son-in-law is cheeky," "she doesn't like me," "there's chaos in traffic," and "I don't feel well" are vague. The therapist can use these as instructive examples to sensitize the client to the importance of precise and corREBT language use. Since language is connected to thinking, accurate phrasing can foster the clarity of the client's thinking. For example, with the statement "My son-in-law is cheeky," the therapist can ask what exactly the son-in-law did that led the client to this conclusion. The statement "She doesn't like me" is similarly unclear. The therapist might ask, "Based on what facts did you conclude that she doesn't like you?" After the client mentions that traffic was chaotic, the therapist can ask, "What happened that made you think traffic was chaotic?" The client may also be unclear about whether they mean they are feeling unwell. The therapist should ask, "When did you realize you weren't feeling well?" Being able to distinguish between abstract and concrete statements enables the therapist to quickly identify unclear expressions. By asking guiding questions, the therapist helps the client recall specific situations. This approach makes it easier for the client to place themselves in the actual context, since they only need to remember what they perceived, thought, and felt during the experience.
3. The therapist should advise the client to focus on only one problem during each session and describe just one activating event. If the client wants to resolve his most important issue, he will be able to identify the event that automatically activates his irrational thinking patterns after a few sessions.

Example: The client tells the therapist that he felt guilty after a soccer match, after loudly insulting and abusing the referee in public. He also states that he was angry with himself at the time because he had lost control in front of so many people. The other fans also started insulting the referee, prompting some to throw their bottles onto the field. One fan hit the referee on the head with a bottle, seriously injuring him. The soccer match had to be stopped. In this case, the therapist should ask: "What did you react to most emotionally?" The therapist lists the possible activating events: "The client insults the referee, the audience joins in the insults, the fans throw bottles onto the pitch, the referee is hit on the head, the referee is seriously injured, or the match has to be stopped."

Assuming the client states that the referee's injury triggered the strongest feelings of guilt, the therapist could ask, "What is going through your mind when you feel guilty when you remember the referee's injury?" If the client answers that they are still angry with themselves, the therapist could ask which of the two emotional problems (feelings of guilt or anger at themselves) they would like to resolve first. If the client chooses feelings of guilt because they are more stressful, the therapist checks whether their anger prevents them from freeing themselves from guilt. If this is the case, the therapist recommends that the client first resolve their anger and then their feelings of guilt. In this instance, anger is the secondary emotional problem. The secondary emotional problem or "symptom stress" should generally be resolved first. Only if the secondary emotional problem is not preventing the client from resolving their primary emotional problem (in this case, guilt) can the therapist accept the client's wish to devote this session to resolving it first.

Should the client describe several activating events during a therapeutic session, he is obviously unable to select the most important one. Such clients often evade the therapist's attempts by using the "Yes, but … " thinking pattern, as in the following example.

T: On one hand, you ask your 90-year-old mother to keep her home tidy, and on the other, you notice that food falls from her mouth again when she eats without noticing! Which is more consistent with reality: the demands you make of your mother to keep her home orderly, or the fact that she can no longer do so? Instead of answering the question, the client goes on:

P: Yes, but...what should I do with my daughter, whose home is just as messy, even though she is young, has enough time, and lives alone?

This is a typical situation therapists encounter. In the example, it is evident that the patient is not only avoiding the answer to the question but is also presenting a new problem with several activating events:

- His daughter's apartment is messy.
- She is still living alone.
- She is young and has enough time to keep the apartment in order.

Helpful Techniques to Identify Activating Events

Working with clients who come to therapy willingly and on their own is most pleasant. However, clients are often referred to treatment by friends or family members. Although these clients accept the fact that they have emotional problems, they often cannot remember a specific situation in which they suffered from the emotional problem. In this case, the therapist may use one of the following procedures:

1. At the end of the first session, the therapist gives the client their first homework assignment. The client should describe their emotional problems in a diary and note when and in which situations or circumstances they occurred. Suppose the client is unwilling or unable to recognize and record the emotional problems and activating events in context. In that case, the therapist instructs them to keep a simple diary of everyday events until the next session. From the diary, the therapist can easily recognize the activating events or situations in which the emotional blockades arise.
2. The therapist can recommend that the client ask his friends, acquaintances, and family members in which situations they have recognized anxiety, anger, or depression in him. He should unconditionally accept his confidants' feedback, make a note of it, and thank them.
3. The therapist can ask the client about their previous day. In doing so, they should mainly indicate activities and situations that they experienced as unpleasant, dull, challenging, stressful, or terrible.
4. The therapist could guide the client through an imagery exercise. The client should imagine a typical situation where most people react with an unhealthy feeling. For example, the client could imagine his wife nagging him or his mother-in-law giving him "smart" advice.

Chapter 11
Agreement on the Therapeutic Goal

Some clients only become motivated to solve their emotional problems when they realize that doing so can help them achieve their goals more quickly and easily. To increase the client's motivation for therapy, the therapist can modify therapeutic goals throughout the session. One important reason for changing the therapeutic goal is if the therapist identifies that a secondary emotional problem is hindering the achievement of the agreed-upon initial therapeutic goal. Another important reason may be that the therapist learns the client has identified a new, even more significant emotional problem that should be prioritized for resolution.

If the therapeutic goal agreed upon with an overweight client is to reduce their body weight, it may emerge during the therapeutic process that the goal of the therapy needs to be changed. For clients to successfully reduce their body weight, they often first need to become aware of their emotional blockages and overcome them. For example, an overweight client may be angry about their previous unsuccessful attempts to lose weight, which often causes them to eat even more to comfort and reassure themselves. Therefore, his anger gets in the way, preventing the client from changing their eating habits to lose weight. Another obstacle to successful weight loss could be low frustration tolerance, which prevents the client from staying disciplined because they think they cannot abstain from their favorite, calorie-dense, and high-sugar foods. A third barrier could be potential feelings of guilt and shame, as they are ashamed of their appearance while simultaneously believing they are responsible for it. They could overcome these barriers by accepting themselves unconditionally, even though they may not like their appearance. As the therapy progresses, it may even turn out that the client is afraid of being unable to do anything to lose weight.

For this reason, they remain in a constant state of anxiety. They can bear this anxiety only by reaching for comforting chocolate and Coca-Cola again and continuing their lives as "couch potatoes." This anxiety and the other barriers mentioned prevent them from concentrating on the practical steps they could take to reduce their body weight. The unpleasant consequences of this include

M. Vlajkov, *Basics of Rational-Emotive Behavior Therapy*,
https://doi.org/10.1007/978-3-032-19448-0_11

continued overeating, avoidance of social contact, and neglect of their bodies. In that case, it is essential first to overcome the emotional barriers mentioned above before the therapist and client turn their attention to changing eating habits and the physical training program (endurance and strength training, as well as fat burning).

The therapist consistently considers the client's long-term goals. Therefore, it is advisable to establish at the beginning of therapy what the client hopes to achieve in the long run and whether the short-term goals align with the client's long-term expectations and wishes. Less experienced therapists may make the following mistakes when setting goals:

1. Instead of educating and empowering the client to free themselves from emotional blockades, the therapist accepts the client's desire to feel just a little less bad or a little less anxious, angry, or depressed. According to the principles of REBT, unpleasant, unhealthy feelings should be replaced by pleasant, yet healthy feelings. The unpleasant, healthy feelings do not block the clients but support them and enable them to deal constructively with difficult life situations. It is also helpful for clients to distinguish and precisely name their feelings. Only then can the client think and speak clearly. These are the basic prerequisites for lasting therapeutic success.
2. The therapist should not give the client the impression that the situations are causing unpleasant, unhealthy feelings by diREBTing the client's attention to this quasi-causality, but should encourage them to feel neutral, in control, or even calm in such situations. If the therapist fails to calm the client down with this clue alone, they should look for ways that would help the client put themselves in a healthy emotional state. The client's statements that indicate the absence of any emotion are more likely to indicate a psychotic disorder than a healthy relationship to life's difficulties. Should the therapist encourage the client to feel indifferent to the frustrating situation, he reinforces the client's belief that one should forgo healthy wishes and resign oneself to life in an apathetic manner rather than actively seeking improvement. If the client permanently renounces their desires, they merely resign themselves to unpleasant situations, and their condition will continue to deteriorate.
   An example of this could be a person with gingivitis. If this person "accepts" their inflammation and even resigns themselves to it, they give up the wish to heal. This then leads them to avoid going to the dentist, and their condition worsens. On the other hand, a person with a strong desire to recover will continue seeking solutions until the cause of the gingivitis is identified and appropriate medical measures are taken.
3. Some therapists believe that there is something positive in every unpleasant event (this is classical positive thinking, which, in the context of positive therapy, is referred to as "healthy optimism"). They believe the client is doing something good for themselves when they find something positive in unpleasant events.

REBT takes a different view: events judged as negative and preventing clients from achieving their goals are labeled as adverse events. However, if the client evaluates them as positive, they reinforce their conviction that they should not be changed. This is an irrational approach to reality. It is an undeniable fact that gingivitis is painful and damages the client—he experiences pain, takes painkillers, his work performance drops, and he loses time due to treatment. The only function of pain is to make people aware of a dysfunction so they can do something about it. Making light of the pain is nothing more than self-comfort, which ultimately has a discouraging effect because the affected person not only resigns themselves to the situation as disadvantageous but even declares it good.

4. Some therapists accept vague goal definitions from their clients. For example, if a client aims to live stress-free, the therapist might ask, "Is it possible to live stress-free?" If the therapist accepts an unrealistic goal instead of asking the question above, they set a trap for themselves. They can only escape this trap by questioning the client's goal and redefining it. Stress is a natural response of the body to an objective or subjective threat, involving hormonal mobilization. The role of stress is to mobilize resources to eliminate the perceived or actual danger. Since neither the therapist nor the client can control the physiological reactions to stress, the goal of living stress-free is unachievable. Therefore, it's recommended that therapists avoid accepting vague goals and instead work with clients to develop specific goals related to real-life situations. The more precisely and clearly the goals are defined, the more motivated the client will be to participate actively in the therapeutic process to achieve them.
5. When the client is asked, "How would you like to feel in the same situation instead?" therapists often hear that the client wants to feel "good and relaxed." Some therapists accept this answer and set it as a goal for the current session. However, this goal cannot be achieved with REBT. For example, a client with social anxiety disorder often models their expectations on their role models. They assume that actors, TV presenters, and skilled university lecturers know no fear and have no stage fright. They believe this is why these individuals communicate easily and playfully with the audience and always enjoy the spotlight. The clients then choose this behavior and the feeling of mastery as their therapy goal. If the therapist agrees, the therapy is likely to fail. Social anxiety disorder is often linked to generalized anxiety disorder. Therefore, therapy can at best replace fear with courage. Over the past 30 years, the author's work has shown that clients respond better to the feeling of courage than to anxiety. Courage is not only empowering but also healthy. If clients are told they can become the hero of their own life, they will be more motivated to pursue courage. This can help them become successful communicators in this emotional state. Only after mastering this role can they truly feel comfortable and even enjoy it. This goes far beyond REBT therapy. As a result, it's rarely possible to achieve a feeling of "well-being" in a standard therapy session. However, the author has found that the goal of well-being can still be reached during an extended session, known

as a "one-session treatment." Combining cognitive and behavioral methods has proven most effective for the following disorders.

a. Specific phobias (Öst, 2014)
b. Social anxiety disorder
c. Obsessive-compulsive disorder
d. Panic disorder

If the therapist uses relaxation methods with clients who have social anxiety disorder, two things can happen. Either the relaxation distracts the client from the anxiety-inducing thoughts that would create fear and panic, or it activates their imagination, intensifying their anxiety. If the client can relax deeply, this is temporarily beneficial for the client because they learn to feel not only free of anxiety but also at ease. However, there is no guarantee that the relaxation methods will help in the long term because they cannot solve the problem causally. The fears with which the client comes to the therapist are not only cognitively caused but also conditioned. The conditioned fear reactions remain even after the client has gained cognitive insight. Only when the therapist is skilled in the final conditioning process (behavioral therapists are well-versed in this) can the treatment of an anxiety disorder be successfully completed.

It has been found that palliative methods, such as relaxation techniques, dampen the client's interest in thoroughly resolving their anxiety so that clients are even less motivated to free themselves from conditioned fears by exposing themselves to the situation.

As a result, they continue to avoid any social situation. In doing so, they ultimately sabotage their recovery (overcoming social anxiety).

6. Some therapists try to establish a good therapeutic relationship with their clients at the beginning, rather than adopting a constructive attitude toward their clients' problems from the start. They believe the clients will then feel good in their company. For this reason, they avoid all questions and subjects that could activate the dysfunctional (irrational) thinking patterns, which would put the client in an unhealthy (dysfunctional) emotional state. However, the therapist should be able to ask the client diREBTly, "What is the very worst thing you fear and want to free yourself from in this session?" This question may induce a strong emotional reaction in the client. Some start to cry, some get angry, and others feel offended or insulted. In that case, the therapist should first address the feelings that arise as a secondary emotional problem.
7. Some therapists show great curiosity even about aspects of their clients' lives that are not relevant to achieving therapeutic goals. It would be better for a therapist not to display any personal curiosity, as this can cause the therapy to become unbalanced and a waste of time. Based on the author's previous experience, this type of curiosity often arises in people with unmet social needs and therapists with limited social skills. Self-management techniques are recommended for these therapists to help them focus on essential therapeutic content and set

appropriate priorities. The key to successful therapy is for the therapist to consistently aim to support and empower the client to improve their life in the long term. A better life is possible if the therapist regularly checks whether current goals align with the client's long-term goals. This alignment then guides the therapy strategy.

Chapter 12
Secondary Emotional Problem (Symptom Stress)

Clients often have secondary emotional problems related to their primary emotional problems. A typical example of this is panic. If a patient is afraid of a heart attack, for example, they may induce a panic attack every time they notice that their heart is beating faster than they think it should. Behind the panic attack is the demand that the heart should not beat so fast. If, despite this demand, the patient's heart starts to race while watching TV in a relaxed state, the patient begins to believe that the feared catastrophe (heart attack) is imminent.

The patient's primary emotional problem in this situation is, therefore, the fear of a heart attack. If the patient has already had a panic attack, after noticing that his heart has started beating faster, he will develop a fear of the "heart pounding" (fear of fear) because he thinks that the heart pounding will cause the panic attack and the heart attack. This is then a fear of a panic attack. This fear is then referred to as a secondary emotional problem or symptom stress. The cause of the secondary emotional problem lies in the client's way of thinking:

"If I panic again, I'm guaranteed to kick the bucket from a heart attack, and I must prevent that at all costs!"

It is of great strategic importance for the therapist to leave the decision about how to solve the problem to the patient at the beginning of the therapeutic session. If, during the session, he realizes that his client feels disturbed by his secondary emotional problem and that this disturbance is preventing him from addressing the primary concern, then the therapist explains to the client that the disturbance related to the secondary emotional problem must first be eliminated so that the primary emotional problem can be solved at all. In the above example of the panic attack, this approach looks like this:

The primary emotional problem is panic, and the secondary emotional problem is the fear of panic, which prevents the client from overcoming the primary problem. So the fear must be overcome first. It is only overcome when the client

M. Vlajkov, *Basics of Rational-Emotive Behavior Therapy*,
https://doi.org/10.1007/978-3-032-19448-0_12

unconditionally accepts their panic, believing it may occur again. Only then can the therapist spend the next session overcoming the panic.

In summary, the handling of primary and secondary emotional problems can be described as follows:

Suppose the therapist finds during a standard psychotherapeutic session that his client has a secondary emotional problem in addition to the primary one. In that case, he asks the client which issue he wants to address first. If the client chooses to work on the primary emotional problem first, the therapist accepts this decision for now. Usually, the client justifies his choice by thinking that if he could free himself from the panic, he would "logically" not be afraid of it. However, in doing so, the client overlooks the fact that he can only free himself from the panic if he is no longer fearful of it and can thus think calmly and clearly about its causes. If the client has a secondary emotional problem, it prevents him from resolving the primary one.

In the following situations, the therapist should clearly point out to the client that secondary emotional problems should be addressed first, followed by the primary ones.

1. Suppose the therapist discovers during the psycho-diagnostic assessment that the secondary emotional problem is preventing the client from resolving the primary emotional problem. Then, the secondary emotional problem hinders the therapeutic process in both the session and everyday life.
2. If, during the psycho-diagnostic assessment, the therapist determines that the secondary emotional problem is more clinically relevant than the primary one. *For example,* the client is a student suffering from reactive depression. He is apathetic, thinks he cannot complete his homework on time, and, as a result, labels himself as incapable. In this case, the secondary emotional problem is depression caused by the student's thinking he shouldn't be so apathetic. This depression is called reactive depression to the primary depression, which the student perceives as apathy. In this example, reactive depression is more clinically relevant than apathy.

Why Is Reactive Depression More Clinically Relevant?

It prevents the student from overcoming his primary depression and worsens his emotional state. It forms the basis for further emotional problems, such as feelings of guilt that arise from attributing his inability to free himself from apathy. Another emotional issue that can develop from this is the fear that he will never recover from his depressive state, which can be terrifying to live with in the long run. The real clinical significance of reactive depression comes from its potential to develop into a severe depressive crisis with suicidal risk. Such cases of suicide or attempted suicide resulting from failure at school or in final university exams are especially well-known among Japanese students.

3. Suppose the client realizes that it makes more sense for him to address the secondary emotional problem first and then focus on the primary emotional problem. In that case, the therapist should acknowledge the patient's insight and agree that resolving this problem should be the initial therapeutic goal.
4. If the therapist recognizes a client's resistance to solving the secondary emotional problem, he should avoid pressuring the client. Instead, he should respect the client's wish and focus on the primary emotional problem. This primary issue is likely unsolvable, which may lead the client to realize that following the therapist's original advice is the best course rather than continuing to resist.

Secondary Emotional Problem

About the Unpleasant Healthy Feelings

A special group of secondary emotional problems involves emotional blockades related to unpleasant healthy feelings. These may have two causes:

1. Low frustration tolerance: Occurs when the client thinks they cannot tolerate an unpleasant but healthy feeling and should not feel uncomfortable in a frustrating situation.
2. Absolutistic perfectionism: This is referred to as EGO anxiety in REBT. This fear arises when the client feels uncomfortable and, at the same time, thinks that they should not feel this way. They see this "discomfort" as a weakness that makes them feel inferior.

Example: If a man is sad because his long-term girlfriend left him for another man, sadness is an unpleasant but healthy feeling. If he is now angry with himself because he feels sad, then the anger toward himself is a secondary emotional problem. The therapist's task is to motivate the client to overcome the secondary emotional problem (anger), but not to free him from sadness, because sadness is a healthy emotional reaction to any loss.

Another secondary emotional problem arises when the client avoids some (for him sensitive) topics in the therapeutic session. If the therapist notices that the client is ashamed to talk about something, he should use the model "What … if … " or "How … if … ": "How would you feel if you had sexual difficulties with your partner?" If the client answers that they would be ashamed to talk about it, then the therapist can recommend overcoming their feelings of shame as a therapeutic goal. This is necessary to enable the client to solve his even more significant emotional problems (than the feeling of shame).

Secondary emotional problems can be addressed quickly, since primary problems always arise in a context with specific activating events that trigger certain thinking patterns, so they should be approached similarly. The therapist can easily identify the thoughts that lead to secondary emotional problems. In a therapy session, the REBT therapist strategically follows these steps:

1. He diagnoses the practical problem, the primary emotional problem, and, if present, the secondary emotional problem.
2. He first solves the secondary emotional problem,
3. Then he solves the primary emotional problem, and finally
4. He gives hints for solving the practical problem.

Example: The client procrastinates on a communication training course that would be important for his professional advancement.

The Diagnosis

1. The client does not know how to properly motivate, inform, stimulate, and control his employees; therefore, he should attend a communication training course.
2. He is worried because he has noticed that his employees are achieving increasingly poor results, and that the company is therefore becoming less able to survive in competition with other companies.
3. The client is angry with himself because he is worried about the situation. He blames himself for not specifically addressing his employees and not criticizing them for their mistakes.

The Secondary Emotional Problem

1. The client realizes that he got upset because he thinks he shouldn't be worried.
2. He accepts that it is human to feel anxious in such a critical situation. This motivates him to act corREBTly.

The Primary Emotional Problem

The client is only "worried," indicating they do not have a primary emotional problem. The "concern" is an unpleasant but healthy feeling.

Practical Tips

The therapist works with the client to identify ways they can improve their communication skills.

a. Assertiveness training: The client decides to tell his employees something uncomfortable every day; in other words, to give them instructions on how to corREBT their mistakes.
b. He registers for a workshop to improve his communication skills.
c. He schedules a "jour fixe" with his employees every Monday.

Chapter 13
The Explanation of the B–C Connection

The key point of REBT is the insight that emotional problems are mainly caused by the way clients think. Some clients can understand the relationship between thinking and feeling based on a precise explanation alone. Others need concrete examples.

If a client doesn't understand how emotional issues develop, they won't grasp the meaning of the therapist's question: What is "going through his mind" when he is overwhelmed by an unhealthy feeling? Therefore, inexperienced therapists should use different convincing examples to explain and clarify the connection between thinking and feeling to their clients.

1. The therapist can explain the relationship between thinking and feeling in different ways: for example, by asking the client whether everyone gets upset when they get stuck in a traffic jam. If the answer is no, the therapist asks the client: "What do you think? How is it that some people get upset in the same situation while others don't?"
2. The next question sensitizes the client even more to the relationship between thinking and feeling: "What does a person who got upset in a traffic jam think, and what does the person who remains relatively calm and listens to the radio in the same situation think?"
3. Another way to explain the relationship between thinking and feeling to the client is through the theoretical model of REBT. The therapist explains the ABC model of feelings to the client and asks them to provide a few examples from their own lives to illustrate it. This triggers the client's "cognitive insight" that unhealthy feelings arise from their thinking.
4. The therapist can show the client that the difference between unpleasant healthy and unpleasant unhealthy feelings diREBTly depends on thinking. Furthermore, he divides the feelings into two categories: pleasant and unpleasant. He then focuses his client's attention on the unpleasant feelings, which he divides into two categories: healthy and unhealthy. Unpleasant healthy and unpleasant

M. Vlajkov, *Basics of Rational-Emotive Behavior Therapy*,
https://doi.org/10.1007/978-3-032-19448-0_13

unhealthy feelings can arise in the same unpleasant situation. If the client thinks rationally, they will develop an unpleasant but healthy emotion that is natural and appropriate to the situation. On the other hand, the unhealthy reaction in the same situation arises solely from irrational thinking.

5. The client can best understand the connection between thinking and feeling if he can recognize himself in the therapist's example. Some "universal" examples follow:

   a. A woman stands at the end of a queue at a supermarket checkout. Other customers gradually joined the queue behind her. Suddenly, a second checkout opens without the woman noticing. She only sees that everyone in line behind her has moved to the second checkout. Now, both queues are the same length, and the woman is once again in last place. She begins to get upset that she hasn't noticed another checkout has opened, that the others are being so rude by jumping the queue, and that she now doesn't know which queue is the "faster" one. She decides to stay in the previous queue, which turns out to be the "slower" one. The therapist asks his client, "Have you ever been in a situation like this? And how would you feel…?"
   b. A man suffers from a fear of flying. His mother is celebrating her 80th birthday in Mallorca and has invited him to join her. She has already booked the ticket and the hotel room. He knows that his mother is not afraid of flying and that she cannot understand how anyone can be fearful of a comfortable plane. The mere idea of taking a plane to Mallorca makes him feel uneasy. The therapist asks his client: "What do you think the man in the example is thinking to produce his fear of flying, and what does his mother, who has never had a fear of flying, think?"
   c. A young woman is about to take a driving test. She has already had three driving instructors and over 50 driving lessons with each of them. She failed the practical test once because she couldn't back up. Although she has practiced parking intensively, she still feels insecure, and when she thinks about the driving test, she is overwhelmed by intense fear. The therapist's question is: "What is going through the young woman's mind to cause her intense fear? What is she imagining? Do you think everyone is afraid of their driving test? Was Michael Schumacher afraid of his driving test, and what was he thinking?"
   d. A man falls madly in love with a woman. After getting together, he realizes she is still actively pursuing the relationship with her "ex." He feels confused, as if he has lost the ground under his feet. He has no appetite, is apathetic and listless, and is constantly tired and tearful. He can no longer work or sleep. Even watching TV and using his cell phone can't distract him. The therapist's question is: "What do you think this man is thinking to make himself suffer like a dog? What is he thinking that makes him feel so depressed? Are there men who think, feel, and behave differently in the same situation?"

e. A driver is overtaken on the right by another driver on the highway. While overtaking, the other driver gives him the "finger." "How do you think the driver who has been overtaken on the right feels after seeing the 'stinky finger' from the speeding driver? How will a foreigner, for example, who doesn't know the meaning of the 'stinky finger' feel? What does a New Zealander think who is constantly overtaken on the right at home when he is driving on the highway—would he also get upset and feel offended?"

Chapter 14
Searching for Irrational Beliefs—B

At this stage of the therapeutic process, the therapist focuses on distinguishing between rational and irrational ways of thinking and explains this to the client: Rational thoughts lead to healthy feelings, while irrational thoughts result in unhealthy feelings. The client needs to learn to identify different types of irrational thinking. Early in therapy, it is less critical but beneficial for the therapist to recognize which irrational thinking patterns underpin the client's emotional problems. Throughout therapy, the therapist will instruct the client on various types of irrational thinking and how to recognize and distinguish them.

Four thinking patterns have been mentioned so far. All four can be applied to three of the client's realities: himself, his fellow humans, and his life circumstances. This results in 12 forms of irrational thinking patterns. They are linked in such a way that one of the thinking patterns can be present in another thinking pattern.

Suppose someone claims that climbing a mountain in a gondola would be terrible. In that case, the therapist has two options: start checking this statement with the client or assume a low frustration tolerance or an absolutistic demand behind these catastrophizing thoughts. It is checked with the question: "And if it were terrible, what would that mean for you?" "I couldn't stand it." So, at the core of the irrational thinking pattern is the thought, "I can't stand it," and the therapist can check it with the client. If the therapist continues to ask, "And what if you can't stand it?" Most clients answer that they must avoid getting into this situation at all costs. This statement is an absolutistic demand, so the therapist can ask the client, "As long as you think that you absolutely have to prevent the gondola ride, and someone forces you to get on the gondola, how would you feel?" The client replies, "As always, when I'm at the airport, I panic." In this example, other thinking patterns could be traced back to an absolutistic demand, but this is not always so. Low frustration tolerance (I can't stand it) is at the root of the fear in the most specific phobias. For some everyday problems (fear that the child will not pay attention to the red light), catastrophizing is a sufficient thinking pattern that can trigger fear and block the client.

M. Vlajkov, *Basics of Rational-Emotive Behavior Therapy*,
https://doi.org/10.1007/978-3-032-19448-0_14

Although Ellis claimed that all emotional problems can be traced back to absolutistic demands, other proponents of cognitive therapy and REBT believe that emotional problems can only be solved if the client recognizes the thinking pattern underlying their suffering. These authors state that there are two levels of therapeutic work in cognitive therapy:

1. The concrete level at which clients replace their concrete thoughts that precede the emotional problem with other thoughts during the therapeutic session.
   To ensure lasting therapeutic success, the therapist then has to raise the client to the next level:
2. The level of abstract thinking. In cognitive therapy, this level is called a cognitive schema. A cognitive schema arises when a client has internalized their dysfunctional thoughts through repetition, making them part of their cognitive design as a thinking pattern (Young, 2005).

For therapeutic success, it is of essential importance that the client understands that their irrational thoughts are the cause of various emotional problems. These irrational thoughts develop when the client turns their wishes and desires into demands. While wishes are flexible and need not always be fulfilled, demands are rigid and do not allow exceptions. If the client doesn't relinquish their absolutist demands, they begin to suffer. Albert Ellis states that such demands are responsible for many emotional disorders and often manifest in the form of derivatives. These derivatives can take various forms.

1. Catastrophizing
2. Low frustration tolerance ("I can't stand it")
3. Labeling or damning
4. Cursing
5. Thinking in extremes: either-or, all-none, always-never, all-nothing, and so on.

Most of the forms of derivatives we are familiar with have already been described in the chapter on thinking errors. When the therapist recognizes these thinking patterns, he should determine which of the three possible absolutistic demands are at their core:

- the demand on oneself,
- the demand on others
- the demand on the circumstances.

Absolutistic demands are usually expressed with the phrase "It should..." Semantically, this phrase implies a conditional demand, but in colloquial language, "it should..." is a hidden absolutistic demand. Therapists are advised to look for statements like "One should...," "One has to...," "I should...," and "I must..." or "I have to..." because these are the easiest ways for them to identify absolutistic demands as the causes of their clients' emotional problems.
Exemples:

- "I have to get to work on time." The client is stuck in a traffic jam and will not arrive at work on time. However, if he constantly thinks he must get to work on time and should not be late, he is in conflict with reality. On the

one hand, he is prevented from being on time, but on the other hand, he demands punctuality.
- A client demands that he not forget his credit card, bank account, and login passwords. As people can always forget something, important information can also be overlooked, especially if they insist on remembering it. Suppose the client mentioned above is unable to recall his credit card PIN, particularly when he wants to withdraw cash from an ATM in a foreign city. In that case, he will most likely be enraged and bang his hand against the screen when his card is "swallowed" by the machine after the third attempt.

The therapist should listen carefully to the client's narrative to notice which of the phrases mentioned above the client uses to express their absolutistic demands. The therapist should develop a particular sensitivity to the following expressions:

1. One should/must; I should/must
2. One shouldn't; I shouldn't/I must not
3. Something is necessary
4. Something is needed, or absolutely needed
5. Absolutely—in the sense of exclusively and urgently
6. Something is essential,
7. Absolute, significant, important
8. vital, essential, indispensable

If the client uses some of these terms, the therapist should spot the context in which they are used. This will allow the therapist to identify the activating events to which the client's demands relate. The therapist should then ask the client how they feel when they think like that. In this way, the therapist establishes a connection between thinking and unhealthy feelings, thereby diverting the client's attention from the activating event, which the client had thought was the cause of their emotional problem. The therapist guides the client towards insight by connecting their thinking patterns to the emotional problem.

In the REBT book The Principles and Practice of Rational-Emotive Therapy (Wessler & Wessler, 1980), the authors state four irrational thinking patterns that cause emotional blockades. In addition to absolutistic demands, they also include global rating, low frustration tolerance, and catastrophizing. The author of this book also agrees with Wessler & Wessler's view and believes that therapy achieves better results when the therapist challenges existing irrational thinking patterns and replaces them with more rational thinking.

How should the therapist proceed to discover and examine these thinking patterns? First, he asks the client which of the following thinking patterns most closely corresponds to his way of thinking:

- Absolutistic demands
- Global rating
- Catastrophizing
- Low frustration tolerance

If necessary, the therapist explains these irrational thinking patterns to the client. The client is free to choose one or more thinking patterns, which are then challenged. The therapist acts as if he is on the same level of knowledge as his client.

An absolutistic demand can be disputed (challenged, checked, questioned) in several ways. One type is the logical dispute, which is based on the principle of consistency. In the context of REBT, something is logical or consequential if it necessarily follows from the premise. The wishes themselves are flexible and do not always have to be fulfilled. If a client thinks he must get to sleep at night or he will not be well-rested in the morning, then his demand is conditional. The difference between a conditional and an absolutistic demand is that the absolutistic demand functions like a physical law in the client's mind. When clients transform their wishes into demands, a blockade arises, especially when these demands cannot be realized. Some people are obsessed with maintaining their health; when the desire to retain it escalates into a demand, they put themselves under enormous pressure. However, the chronic stress that results from this is, in turn, detrimental to maintaining health. It is, therefore, desirable to convert the demands back into wishes. An absolutistic demand is examined within a logical dispute when clients are asked the question: "Just because you wish for something, does it automatically follow that this wish must be fulfilled?." This logic can be clearly seen in an example:

If someone thinks, "I want to stay healthy, and therefore, I must always manage to stay healthy," this last part is an absolutistic demand that is like a law of the Universe in the client's mind. However, it is only a wish and not a natural law. We will discuss the logical dispute in more detail later.

A global assessment is an abrupt conclusion about a whole (relating to people, facts, circumstances, or oneself) based on the little available evidence.

For example, it is common to call a person who frequently lies a liar, or a person who behaves maliciously toward others a malicious person. The same is true of a person who commits a crime and is called a criminal.

A simple question can easily challenge the global rating as a form of irrational thinking: "How does it follow from the fact that someone has lied several times that they are a liar?" When this statement is made, it suggests that the other person has never told the truth and will continue to lie. If this person were to say to themselves, "I am a liar," it would be considered true. But if the liar said, "This is my only truth," that would also be false, since he can never tell the truth, being a liar. A repeated act cannot turn a person into someone else.

The rational way of thinking is that one only evaluates and describes what can be measured or described. In disputes with the client, the global rating is often questioned as dysfunctional thinking:

T: "What do you think of a rose that smells nice?"

(Most people admire this beautiful rose scent.)

T: "Is the rose itself beautiful and good?"

(Most clients would say "yes," and then the therapist replies:)

T: "Does the rose have thorns?"

K: "Yes."

Just as a rose has thorns on the outside, a person cannot be equated with their appearance, behavior, or temperament.

The client should understand that an offensive remark does not make a person bad or a "stupid dog." Most people resist challenging their global ratings because they are socially justified. Broadly evaluating others helps us to navigate the social environment more easily. It is wise to question this overall rating and replace it with rational thinking only when such a global assessment leads to hatred, or triggers anger or fear.

After the Industrial Revolution, the quality of life improved in Western nations and, increasingly, in the Far East—Japan, China, Australia, New Zealand, and so on—so only a few people lack a livelihood. Food, sleep, security needs, maintaining body temperature, and social norms enable everyone to live a safe and comfortable life. Suffering from anxiety in these circumstances is primarily caused by the anxious person's thinking. For example, if a person imagines a catastrophe from a minor inconvenience they have experienced, this can cause great fear. In some cultures, the worst curse is to wish someone first to have something and then lose it. The person who has lost perceives this loss as heavier than the one who has nothing to lose. Anyone who turns a harmless, unpleasant event into a catastrophe will gradually develop a strong fear of loss. In cognitive therapy, the counteracting process is called decatastrophizing. This process is described in detail in this book in the section on challenging irrational beliefs.

The low frustration tolerance arises from the client's assertion that they cannot stand something. After humans have satisfied their basic needs, there is hardly anything that people can't endure. The elegant way to explain the thinking pattern that creates low frustration tolerance is: "If they were to expose themselves to this circumstance, would they stand it or die from it?" Most clients answer that they have never died from it, but that they still can't stand it. Suppose the therapist offered them the right way of thinking, like "I can understand that it would be difficult for you because you don't like it and it is unpleasant or challenging, even very hard, but that is not proof that you can't endure it." In that case, that's when the client realizes their statement is exaggerated and inconsistent with reality and the facts.

How can the therapist discover the specific thinking pattern from which the acute emotional problem arises? The therapist has two options:

1. During the therapy session, when the client is clearly overwhelmed by an unhealthy feeling, the therapist asks: "What do you think about when you feel like this, or what is going through your mind when you cry, or what thoughts have made you feel so angry(in this concrete situation)?" This helps prevent the client from giving an assumed or made-up answer. Unskilled therapists ask clients: "What goes through your mind when you feel anxious?" These questions are inadequate because they do not refer to a specific situation in which the client can remember their thoughts.
2. If the therapist has diagnosed that the client suffers from anxiety, then he asks: "When did you last feel your anxiety?" "When, how, and where did this happen? In which situation?" The client describes a situation, the time, and what the fear

looked like. The therapist then asks them, for example: “When you were overwhelmed by anxiety at work two days ago, what went through your mind? What did you think?” Most clients can easily remember the thoughts that put them in an anxious state. These thoughts were emotionally conditioned, and this type of learning is called emotional learning or “learning all at once.”

3. The best way to demonstrate how to identify the thought that triggered the emotional problem is with the following example:

The therapist asks his patient:

T: “When was the last time you felt depressed (angryor anxious?”

P: "Yesterday morning, after I woke up.”T: "What happened?”

P: “I saw the cloudy sky through the bedroom window.”

T: ” How did you feel about that?”

P: “Depressed, gloomy, and sad.”

T: What were you thinking then? What was going through your mind at that emotional moment?

P: I'm a poor soul; I can't look forward to anything; I need light to feel better. Always this lousy German weather! It’s just bad weather all the time.

In this way, the therapist understands the actual thoughts and hears the diREBT cause of emotional disturbances. This increases the chance that therapy will succeed. Through this method, the therapist sensitizes the client to the fact that thoughts lead to emotional problems. The patient then recognizes the importance of examining irrational beliefs. Metaphors can help make the therapy more effective. If someone suffers from anger attacks, they can think about them in two ways.

1. External circumstances cause anger.
2. He put himself in an angry state.

If he believes the circumstances are responsible for his fits of anger, he has no way to avoid them. However, if he thinks he is putting himself into an angry state, he can also calm down and free himself from the anger. A television set and a remote control serve as ingredients for a metaphor to illustrate this for the client. The client represents the television set, and the remote control symbolizes the trigger of their anger. Suppose the remote control is in someone else’s hands. In that case, this person can “press the buttons” and elicit an angry reaction (or any other feeling) and “select” a particular program. However, the client can also take the remote control into their own hands and set their own “programs.” Then comes the question: “Who is supposed to press the buttons on the remote control?” The answer is left to the reader.

The use of examples can also be highly beneficial: imagine a client whose parents died long ago. The client comes to therapy because he cannot free himself from his anger towards his parents. They didn’t allow him to study English abroad decades ago. Although he had completed his English studies in Germany, he has still not managed to overcome his anger towards his parents. The client faces the choice of accepting the decision his parents made many years ago as a given or continuing to ruminate on why they did not allow him to study abroad at the time, even though he wanted it so much. If the client realizes in therapy that he is causing his anger at his parents himself, then he will be able to free himself from the anger.

Chapter 15
Wishes, Preferences, Conditional and Absolutistic (Unconditional) Demands

In the context of REBT, the statement "Should" is understood in two different ways. The first refers to "preferential thinking," and the second to "absolutistic demands." When the word "should" is used in the preferential sense, it can be replaced with the phrase "it would be desirable" and refers to recommendations for a particular way of behaving and thinking. Additionally, the term "preferential thinking" expresses prioritizing one issue over another. If a client is forced to choose between two unpleasant situations (e.g., painful dental treatment versus a permanent toothache), they might prefer the option they consider less disadvantageous. However, it cannot be said that the client truly wants either of these options. Typically, people wish for a new car, a beautiful wife, a lovely apartment, or good health. On the other hand, no one would want a surgical operation, but this operation is preferable to a lifetime of pain.

In the second case, the verb "ought to" expresses a hidden demand. The demand can be conditional or unconditional (absolutistic). Conditional demands are used as a therapeutic tool with clients who have emotional blockades in relation to the goal to be achieved. Example: A client applies for a job advertised. He thinks he absolutely has to get this job because he meets all the requirements. A few days later, he received an invitation to an interview. From this moment on, he begins to suffer from stage fright. He is aware that other candidates have also applied for this job and that he may therefore be rejected. In this case, he can use two meanings of "should":

1. The potential employer ought to hire me because I am the best candidate.
2. The potential employer should hire me because I am the best candidate.

In the first case, it is a hidden unconditional (absolutistic) demand. In the second case, the meaning of the demand is softened by the conditional form of the verb. This conditional form shows the condition under which the demand is justified and can be fulfilled, but it does not have to be fulfilled.

M. Vlajkov, *Basics of Rational-Emotive Behavior Therapy*,
https://doi.org/10.1007/978-3-032-19448-0_15

However, if the applicant understands the term "preferential should" as an absolutistic demand (which is often the case), he or she will continue to suffer from stage fright and likely perform worse in the interview than their actual abilities and potential warrant.

If, on the other hand, he can clearly experience the difference between "should" and "ought" emotionally, then the conditional demand will transform his stage fright, which was inhibiting him up to this point, into a beneficial stage fright. This enables him to perform better at the interview and significantly increases his chances of getting the job. The sentence "I must get this job!" is an absolutistic demand, as it doesn't contain any condition under which it can be fulfilled. This unfulfillable demand intensifies stage fright. If the applicant thinks, "I should get this job!" then this statement contains at least one condition under which he could get it. The unspoken condition is: "If I want to get this job, then I must prepare for the interview (have a good night's rest, drink coffee, have a well-groomed appearance, show myself in my best light, and have under control everything I can influence). However, I may not get the job because the company may choose someone else, not me." In REBT, this is a functional, conditional demand and is referred to as rational belief.

As has already been mentioned several times, Albert Ellis argues that every form of emotional disorder is based on absolutistic demands. The goal of every REBT therapy is to change an unhealthy feeling into a healthy emotional state. This happens by unmasking the absolutistic demands that have caused unhealthy feelings. Ultimately, it is up to the therapist and their client to transform the irrational demands into rational statements. Since the patient often expresses their absolutistic demands as preferences or conditional demands, the therapist should unmask hidden demands, make them understandable to the client, check them with the client for validity and truth, and replace them with rational beliefs.

Furthermore, during the therapy, the therapist may also be confronted with other forms of irrational beliefs that cannot be traced back to absolutistic demands. These include catastrophizing, global ratings, and low frustration tolerance.

It often happens that the client only names so-called derivatives (derivations from irrational core beliefs). He does not recognize that these derivatives are based on absolutistic demands. In this case, the therapist should check the derivatives with the client; they will be proven to be false. Checking, that is, challenging the derivatives, is an inductive procedure. Clients gain several "small" insights, which gradually transform their unhealthy feelings into healthy ones.

Example: A client suffers from lovesickness and seeks a therapist to help him overcome it. During the first therapeutic session, the therapist realizes that the client cannot see that his absolutistic demand ("She must love me and come back to me!") is the cause of his heartache. During the session, other beliefs of the client emerge that are diREBT causes of his heartache.

- "She has let me down!"
- "She took advantage of me!"
- "She just leaves me hanging!"

- I'm a broke bastard!
- If only she were with me, everything would be fine again!
- and so on.

Each of these statements can be verified for accuracy from the perspective of the cognitive approach. "She left me in the lurch!" can be analyzed by asking whether she fell in love with someone else or left him to harm him. Are there actually facts to support his claims, or are they just general assumptions? The client usually responds cooperatively and rationally, reaching the conclusion that his allegation is merely an assumption (hypothesis). An assumption also includes other possibilities. For example, his "ex" could have felt constrained by him and therefore left him. She would have left him not because of him but because of herself, so his original assumption lessens its impact on his heartache, and he begins to suffer less. In this way, every previously mentioned derivative can be questioned and corREBTed. This process is called "cognitive corREBTions."

However, suppose another client can understand the relationship between a derivative and the absolutistic demand on which it is based. In that case, the therapist should lead him to the insight that the absolutistic demand has caused suffering. In the example of the "three red traffic lights" mentioned above, the therapist does this as follows:

When you think about being slowed down by a red wave and feel that it's not okay for you, how does that make you feel? The client first responds, "Of course, it's not okay that I have to stop so often, and, of course, I freak out!" The therapist then challenges the client with the corresponding absolutistic demand: "The traffic lights should be adjusted so they don't obstruct traffic but keep it flowing!" This client can recognize and resolve the core of the problem by giving up his absolutistic demand and replacing it with a rational statement, without even considering the derivatives. This process is known as an "elegant solution."

Rational statements that correspond to the form of preferential thinking take the following forms:

- "It would be nice."
- "It would be desirable."
- "I would like it."
- "I wish for it."

In the above example, the rational statement is: "I wish I had a green wave all the time, but if I don't have a green wave, then I don't have to have one!"

Chapter 16
Inference Chaining

When searching for irrational thinking patterns, it is more efficient and safer to ask the client what he is thinking rather than simply assuming which irrational thought pattern underlies his current emotional problem. The best moment to recognize the client's irrational thinking pattern is when the client understands the B–C connection. The therapist then asks the client, "When was the last time you felt like this?" The client usually remembers the moment he felt blocked. The therapist then asks, "What happened then?" The patient describes the whole event.

The therapist has three possible questions with which he tries to discover the irrational thought pattern:

1. "What was going through your mind while you felt like that?"
2. "What were you thinking about when you felt like that?"
3. "What thoughts did you have to put yourself in this emotional state?"

Example: The client recalls coming home from work and realizing that his child hasn't done his homework on time. The therapist then asks: "How did you feel when you heard that from your child?" The client replies: "Of course, I freaked out first!" The therapist then asks: "What did you think when you were overwhelmed by rage?" He could ask even more precisely and concretely: "What thoughts did you have to get yourself into this rage?"

At this point, it should be explained why a therapist should formulate different questions. Especially if one's questioning technique is superior, better therapeutic results can be achieved. There are several reasons for this:

1. If the therapist repeatedly uses the same phrasing, the client will get used to it. This can lead to boredom and distraction.
2. The therapist would also find repeating the same formulation with many clients and sessions monotonous. As a result, they would be unable to fully concentrate on the therapeutic process.

M. Vlajkov, *Basics of Rational-Emotive Behavior Therapy*,
https://doi.org/10.1007/978-3-032-19448-0_16

3. In some cases, during the therapeutic process, a simpler formulation of the questions may make sense if it is more understandable or "natural" for the client. The same can occur if the question does not include everything that could be asked from a theoretical perspective.
4. Different question formulations require the therapist to think along and actively engage in the therapeutic process.
5. In addition, through different question formulations, the client is motivated to participate in the therapeutic process and engage with the therapy.
6. By using different questioning techniques, the therapist can better manage the therapy. In this sense, therapy can be compared to juggling. Although it requires precision, it is also a relationship between two people. People are constantly changing, as is the context in which the therapy takes place.

The ideal way to formulate a question that can draw out irrational thinking patterns should include three components:

1. The situation in which the patient first became aware of his emotional problem.
2. The emotional problem itself.
3. The thought that caused the emotional problem.

A question that includes all these components aims to help the client recognize the B–C connection.

Another way to identify irrational beliefs involves using a question formulation based on REBT's theoretical concept. There are several types of this questioning method; two will be explained here. The first type relates to the client's demands. In the example mentioned earlier, the therapist should ask the client: "What do you demand from your child while you are angry with them?" The second type of question, guided by REBT theory, concerns a person's global rating. In this case, the therapist asks: "What do you think about your child when you are angry that they haven't done their homework yet?" In the first scenario, the question aims to reveal the client's rigid demand ("The child should have done the homework"). In the second scenario, the focus should be on the client's broad judgment ("The child is an undisciplined slacker").

A less experienced therapist asks a question based on REBT theory, even if they do not yet know whether the client is in a healthy or unhealthy emotional state. The result is that the client responds through an irrational thinking pattern, even if it may not have clinical significance. Therefore, the therapist needs to determine whether the client has a clinically significant emotional problem caused by irrational thinking before searching for irrational thinking patterns.

This leads to the next step: the therapist explains to the client the connection between the irrational belief and the emotional problem, using the client's example. The procedure for identifying irrational thinking patterns is known as inference chaining. This procedure corresponds to a technique in cognitive therapy called the "vertical arrow technique." It assumes that specific thoughts expressed by the client while in an unhealthy emotional state arise from their irrational thinking patterns. Initially, neither the client nor the therapist is aware of these patterns.

The therapist then asks further questions based on known facts to uncover these thinking patterns. The REBT therapist proceeds similarly to a researcher seeking to trace the spring of a newly discovered river, following its course upstream until he reaches the spring. The therapist asks questions in dialogue with the client. Based on the last answer received, he moves toward the "spring" (the irrational thinking pattern). He continues this process until he has clearly identified the irrational thinking pattern.

It is important to emphasize that, for the therapist, identifying the irrational thinking pattern based on clues is crucial, as clients are often unable to express it diREBTly. In this situation, the therapist acts like a detective, combining the client's statements and placing them in context until the underlying irrational thinking pattern emerges. How can the therapist clearly recognize the irrational thinking pattern in an inference chain?

This can be illustrated using a few examples:

Example 1: A client seeks help to improve his relationship with his wife. Due to work, they live apart during the week and see each other only on the weekends.

He has been trying to improve the relationship for years, but has not succeeded, and feels desperate about it. At the beginning of therapy, he was diagnosed with reactive depression. When asked, "When was the last time you felt desperate?" he replies, "Last weekend, when I was talking to my wife about moving into my apartment. She categorically refused to move. That hit me like a knife in the heart! Since then, I haven't felt like working, reading, or entertaining myself; I don't feel like doing anything!"

T: "When your wife refused to move, what did you think?"
K: "How can she do this to me?"

The reader's task is to identify the irrational thinking pattern in the client's response. The client did not ask himself, either out of neutrality or out of curiosity (simply seeking understanding), why his wife acted that way or whether her behavior was diREBTed at him. By asking this question, he is essentially expressing a hidden absolutistic demand to his wife: that she shouldn't have refused to move and shouldn't have hurt him.

T: "And while you think your wife shouldn't have refused to move, how do you feel?"
K: "I am desperate and helpless."

This establishes the link between the irrational thinking pattern and the unhealthy feeling, thus achieving the goal of inference chaining.

Example 2: A client has attended all her psychology degree lectures and has nearly completed all her exams. Only the final thesis and the final exam remain. She states that her professor has called her incompetent and predicted she will never finish her studies. She feels hurt, humiliated, and angry at the professor. When asked what she wants to achieve through this therapy, she says she wants to pass the final exam, complete and submit the thesis, but her feelings of hurt and humiliation are stopping her from doing so.

She says that she feels overwhelmed by anger and a desire for vengeance whenever she thinks about her thesis. She imagines what she could say to her professor to make him feel even worse than she does. When asked, "What is going through your mind when you feel angry and furious with the professor?" she responds, "He's a mean and primitive scumbag. He behaves like a pig toward me!"

T: "And let's assume he really did behave so disrespectfully towards you; what does that mean for you, and what does it say about him?"
K: "That he's a bastard and shouldn't have said something like that to me!"
T: "And as long as you think he's a bastard, how does that make you feel?"
K: "I'm shaking with rage, and I'd love to beat him up!"

In this example, the author illustrates the typical formulation for starting inference chaining. The client names the first thought that comes to her mind when she is gripped by anger. Each client's answer serves as a starting point for formulating the next question. For example, if the client asks, with great astonishment, "Can you imagine that he actually said to me that I am incapable and stupid?" then the therapist replies, "And if he actually said that, what does that mean for you?"

K: "How could he possibly... How could he allow this to himself...?"
And let's say he took the freedom to act that way, what does that mean to you?
K: "That he's a stupid cow! How can he?"
T: And as long as you think he's a bovine, how do you feel?
K: "I'm about to freak out!"

Once the irrational thought pattern has been identified—specifically as a global rating—the therapist begins exploring this thinking pattern with the client.

Chapter 17
Dispute—Review of Irrational Thinking Patterns

Suppose the client recognizes that challenging her irrational thinking pattern and replacing it with a rational one makes sense. In that case, the therapist restates the irrational thought that is causing the client's emotional problem. For example, the therapist repeats the previous statement: "He shouldn't have told me that I'm incompetent and stupid!" This statement is examined during this therapy phase using different criteria. The client should see that this way of thinking does not help her; on the contrary, it harms her. The consequences are that she fails to reach her goals, cannot solve everyday problems, and suffers from long-term chronic stress. The therapist demonstrates that her way of thinking is illogical because she turns her wishes into absolutistic demands, which do not match reality since the facts contradict them.

Therefore, the conclusion is that it would be better for the client to replace her dysfunctional thoughts with rational ones. This would then free her from all the stated problems.

M. Vlajkov, *Basics of Rational-Emotive Behavior Therapy*,
https://doi.org/10.1007/978-3-032-19448-0_17

Chapter 18
The Absolutistic Demands and Their Questioning

The REBT approach argues that absolutistic demands are the most critical irrational thinking patterns. The author's practice, and that of many of his colleagues, has shown that absolutistic demands are the easiest to question. Paradoxically, most clients are unwilling to replace irrational thinking patterns with rational ones, even after gaining cognitive insight.

The procedure for disputing irrational thoughts is as follows:

1. The therapist should agree with the client on the corREBT formulation of the irrational thought pattern to be disputed. Examples of this are:
   T: "How do you feel about your boss not approvingYour vacation in July and August, while thinking that he should approve it?"
   K: "I'm mad at him!"
   T: "Does it make sense to you now that your thinking is causing the anger?"
   K: "That makes sense to me."
   T: "How do you feel as long as you think you should have thanked your mother-in-law for the gift?"
   K: "I feel guilty."
   T: "So your guilt stems from your demand that you should have thanked your mother-in-law."
   K: "That's right."
   T: "How do you feel when you think your professor shouldn't have given you a bad grade without justification?"
   K: "I'm angry that I was mistreated!"
   T: "The thought that you shouldn't have been mistreated is obviously the cause of your anger."
   K: "That's right."

M. Vlajkov, *Basics of Rational-Emotive Behavior Therapy*,
https://doi.org/10.1007/978-3-032-19448-0_18

In all the examples provided, the therapist has identified a diREBT link between the absolutistic demand and the unhealthy emotion. When the client recognizes this connection, it is called cognitive insight. Only then does the client begin to understand how the therapy works.

1. In the next phase, the therapist suggests that the client challenge the absolutistic demand. There are four criteria according to which the absolutistic demands can be questioned. These are:
   a. Usefulness
   b. Logical consistency
   c. Feasibility
   d. Consistency with the facts

(a) *Usefulness:* It is relatively simple to determine whether an irrational thought pattern benefits the client. The therapist asks the client what their way of thinking does for them. The client recognizes that their thinking often harms them, but they also claim that this irrational thinking keeps them motivated to reach their goals. Some clients resist seeing their thinking as harmful because they argue that doing so would mean giving up the goal they want to achieve. They do not understand that if they let go of their absolutistic demands, they would be more motivated rather than overly motivated. Of course, the client's conclusions are wrong because they have already admitted that their absolutistic demands cause emotional blockades. Now, the therapist faces two conflicting statements from the client. He presents both to help the client see the contradiction. This is a case of cognitive dissonance, where the client believes their irrational thinking is both harmful and helpful at the same time. The therapist asks: "How can that be?" He encourages the client to think actively so they realize they only face two bad choices. One is to keep practicing irrational thinking, staying highly motivated, but sabotaging their performance with internal pressure, leading to worse results. The other is to give up their motivating thoughts, stop achieving things, live without pressure, but risk being seen as lazy. To help resolve this inner conflict, the therapist tells the client, "Let's assume for a moment that your demands motivate you to reach your important goals. Would it be better for you to stay highly motivated while freeing yourself from the harmful effects of absolutistic demands? If you truly believe your demands are responsible for your motivation, try saying it one hundred times and see if your motivation significantly increases!" Another way to help the client see why their thinking is harmful is to list all the effects of their unhealthy feelings. As defined earlier, unhealthy feelings cause mental blockades, emotional suffering, counterproductive behaviors, low motivation, and psychosomatic problems.

(b) *Logical consistency (consequentiality)* is tested by asking: "Is it logical to think that just because you want something, you necessarily must have/achieve/get it?" Many clients agree with this logic. In the second step, the therapist provides various examples, clarifying that having a wish does not automatically mean it must be fulfilled.

- A 70-year-old alcoholic wants to pass a driving test. His hands are shaking, his eyesight is poor, and he smells of alcohol. If he now turns his desire into a demand that he must get a driver's license, is his thinking consequent (logical)?
- Someone has the desire to fly like a bird. Is it logical to think that he must succeed when he waves his arms just because he desires to fly like a bird?
- Do you have to win the lottery just because you want to?

(c) *Feasibility:* An absolutistic demand only causes an unhealthy feeling if it cannot be fulfilled. A typical example is when someone demands that a past event should not have happened, or should have happened differently, or should have happened by any means. These examples help the client realize that their demand cannot be fulfilled and that it is better to abandon it rather than keep insisting and "running their head against the wall." The absolutistic demand the client makes about the future (that everything must happen exactly as they want) is hard to verify because the therapist logically has no reliable data from the client's future.

How Should the Therapist Assess Their Client's Absolutistic Demands About the Future?

He again takes on the role of a detective and looks for evidence that speaks against this absolutistic demand. For example, suppose a client demands that his wife return to him, even though she has fallen in love with another man and has been living with him for five years. In that case, the therapist can look for evidence that speaks against the feasibility of the absolutistic demand as follows: "If you wish right now for this glass on the table to lift off and float in the air, would you be able to do that? Can you please try that now?" The client replies, "That's not possible!" "But if there was only a light feather on the table, could you do the trick?" If the client answers in the affirmative, the therapist plucks a single hair from his head, places it on the table, and politely asks his client to demonstrate the power of his demands by moving the hair lying on the table a fraction of a millimeter. Of course, the client quickly realizes that this will not work. Then comes the therapist's crucial question: "How heavy is your wife, how tall is she, and how far away is she? Does she want to come back to you, or stay with the other man? Can you put your absolutistic demand into practice, or does it only create false hope and a depressive mood in you?"

As long as the client maintains his absolutistic demands and continues trying to implement them, he is constantly harming himself. The evidence shows that absolutistic demands have no power to realize themselves (see the example with the hair).

(d) *Consistency with the facts (reality):* The consistency between the irrational absolutistic demand and the facts can be checked by the therapist asking the client whether he has ever been confronted with unfulfilled demands up to now.

When confronting the client about his cognitive dissonance, the therapist explains it and how it can be resolved.

How Can This Cognitive Dissonance Be Resolved?

There are five (auto)destructive and one constructive way of dealing with cognitive dissonance. This process is explained using an example:

A therapist treats a smoker who wants to free himself from his addiction. On the one hand, he knows that smoking harms him and his family, but on the other hand, he claims that smoking gives him pleasure and helps him reduce his stress. He also states that thoughts of pro and contra-smoking worry him because they make him aware of his conflicting attitudes towards smoking. He takes this as an opportunity to light up the next cigarette to calm down again. The conflict between the client's two contradictory attitudes can be resolved in the following five destructive ways:

a. The smoker is not prepared to give up his destructive attitude; therefore, he constantly tries to justify it. For example, the smoker explains that thinking about smoking makes him uncomfortable because, in that case, it makes him aware of his conflicting thoughts about smoking. He then uses this as a reason to take the next cigarette to calm himself down. In doing so, he temporarily overcomes his cognitive dissonance by choosing to smoke and ignoring his reasoning.
b. The smoker can devalue all the facts speaking against smoking by asking: "Who knows how this research was conducted and how the facts were gathered? Maybe an ecological institute 'ordered' these results and financed the research?" The smoker continues smoking with a clear conscience.
c. The smoker looks for facts that speak against the harmful effects of smoking. For example, he mentions former German Chancellor Helmut Schmidt, who lived to be 97 and smoked for most of his life. Or he cites Fidel Castro as his role model, who even smoked cigars and lived to 89. In this case, too, the smoker takes a calm puff on his cigarette.
d. Smokers can also overcome their cognitive dissonance by indefinitely postponing its resolution. He justifies this postponement by saying that he does not have time to stop smoking now. He then takes 5 minutes to "have another smoke."
e. The fifth and final harmful way of coping with cognitive dissonance is to recognize the advantages of the "harmful" attitude. He claims: "Smoking is fun, I enjoy it and don't feel any negative effects, I'm fit!"

The only constructive way to overcome cognitive dissonance is to orient oneself by the facts and adjust one's thinking accordingly. An ex-smoker who has freed himself from his cigarette addiction reports the following in his diary:

Smoking obviously has harmful effects and side effects. That's why I should quit, even if it's tough for me—the side effects of smoking start to show early in the morning when a cough wakes me up. Then I begin coughing nonstop, and a thick phlegm comes up from my lungs. Sometimes, I have to chew this phlegm in my mouth because I can't spit it out. I'm then forced to swallow it, which causes stomach and digestive problems. It makes me feel bloated. I often have to burp and hiccup. Sleeping is impossible. What's worse, the taste in my mouth is disgusting. I can't stand myself, which quickly drives me to light my first cigarette. Then my misery ends for the time being! My tongue hasn't been able to taste anything for years; it's furry and numb from smoking. When I hear others describe what they ate and how it tasted in their chosen words, I can't relate. I know that nine out of ten people who die from lung cancer are smokers (I'm unsure about the one non-smoker who may be a passive smoker). Walking with my friends, I get tired quickly and often run out of breath. The non-smokers hurry ahead and leave me behind, promising to meet me at the pub, "At three donkeys." This is our favorite pub. Over time, I realized why there are only two donkeys on the sign above the door. The third one is obviously me, standing underneath and smoking.

Cognitive dissonance manifests itself not only in the form of absolutistic demands but also in other irrational thinking patterns. When examining absolutistic demands, the therapist should proceed with the following questions:

1. "Is it useful for you to think this way, and accordingly, what do you gain from this way of thinking?"
2. "Have you always succeeded in making your absolutistic demands work so far?"—This question is asked when the client has demands about their future. If the client insists that they must change the past, the therapist uses the following phrasing: "As long as you think you should have thanked your mother-in-law for the gift, do you really believe that this thought can change the past, as if you could travel back in time with a time machine to change things that happened?"
3. "Is it logical that if you wish for something, you must automatically get/or achieve it?" An alternative question is: "How can the necessity follow from your wish alone that it must be fulfilled?" "Is there any evidence to the contrary?" "Have you ever wished for something that was not fulfilled?"

Obviously, the past cannot be changed, so it is illogical to insist it should have been different. It is advisable not only to challenge irrational thoughts through the questions mentioned, but also to bring the client to insight through examples that point to the dysfunctionality of their irrational thoughts. This approach increases the client's willingness to accept a rational way of thinking.

Immediately after disputing irrational beliefs, the therapist determines whether the client is ready to give up their previous way of thinking and replace it with a rational one. The formulation of rational beliefs then follows this.

A rational belief consists of three parts:

1. Wish
2. Fact
3. Acceptance

In the first part, the client formulates his own wish. In doing so, he returns to his original wish and gives up the absolutistic demand that arose from it. How can the client be brought to give up his absolutistic demand and recognize in his inner self that it is wrong?

The therapist and the client list the facts that speak against the absolutistic demand. This automatically leads to the third part of the rational formulation—acceptance. The client admits that things can be exactly the way they are, rather than insisting they shouldn`t be as they are.

This phase of therapy is probably the most delicate, as many therapists are often hesitant to confront the client with the opposite of their demand. They adopt a comforting, understanding attitude toward the client, which raises questions about the therapy's ultimate success. If the therapist asks the client, "With what statement can you finally give up your absolutistic demand?" the client usually responds, "It can be the way it is." If the therapist accepts this answer as corREBT, then he has made a serious mistake during the therapy. By using the word "can," the client only reluctantly gives up his demand, and genuine acceptance does not happen. This formulation can also signal to the therapist that the answer is just lip service and that the emotional change the therapy aims for has not yet been achieved.

If the therapist hears from the client that it can be the way it is, then he should replace this "can" with "may" and completely reformulate the complete rational statement:

- "I wish I had thanked my mother-in-law (wish), but since I didn't thank her (fact), I didn't have to thank her (acceptance).

The therapist continues the process by asking, "Which part of this statement don't you like?" Most clients say that they are bothered by the last part of the rational formulation ("That it is allowed to be the way it is."). They interpret this as a general "permission" for their unwanted behavior (or situation). The therapist then replies: "Can we question this part that you don't like and don't yet agree with in terms of usefulness, consistency, and feasibility? You might then experience the rational formulation emotionally. So, why didn't you have to say thank you when you didn't do it?" Many clients then start to laugh because they realize the futility of their stubborn insistence on the absolutistic demand. This means the therapy's desired goal has been achieved.

To clarify this to the client, the therapist asks one last question: "And if you think like this (rationally), how do you feel?" The answer is usually: "I feel relieved, but I'm not happy with it." The therapist recognizes "I'm not happy about it" as an unpleasant but healthy feeling. He then explains to his client that "not being happy" is the desired and appropriate emotional response corresponding to the situation. This can lead the client to behave properly: he apologizes to his mother-in-law and expresses his regret for not having thanked her.

The case described above illustrates how the therapist handles an absolutistic demand on the past. If the client makes an absolutistic demand on the future or a demand on himself about how he should behave in the future, then the following alternative way of thinking is implemented:

Example: A dentist is afraid of not treating her patients satisfactorily. She expects herself to work flawlessly and faultlessly (not to make the slightest mistake). The therapist has worked out a rational alternative with her, which looks like this:

- If I want to work flawlessly, I still have to learn a lot and gain experience. If I still make unintentional mistakes, this shows I don't have to prevent myself from making them.

Her anxiety led her to avoid challenging tasks and only complete routine ones. As a result, she couldn't learn anything or gain new experience. In this case, the absolutistic demand ("I must not make any mistakes") was replaced with a conditional demand ("If I don't want to make any mistakes, I have to learn more and gain more experience!").

Chapter 19
Catastrophizing and Questioning the Catastrophizing

The irrational way of thinking, known as catastrophizing in this chapter, is exemplified by the following statements:

- "It's terrible."
- "It's horrible."
- "It's awful."
- "It's catastrophic."
- "It's dreadful."
- "It's a disaster."

These statements can refer to oneself, other people, and life circumstances.

It is well known that there are three levels of augmentation for the word "bad" (bad, worse, worst). If the client says something is "terrible," the therapist asks him what the augmentation of "bad" is. If the client cannot spontaneously list "worse" and "the worst" on his own, the therapist will help him by offering both options. The client will accept the suggestions, and this alone can lead to a small insight that he is exaggerating in his way of thinking.

This phenomenon is known in psychology as "priming." Through priming, the therapist prepares the client for the next explanation. The therapist asks:

T: "Where would you place the word 'terrible' in the order 'bad-worse-worst' according to your emotional perception?"
K: "Behind the term 'worst'!"
T: "On a scale of 0%–100%, where is 'worst' on this scale?"
K: "At 100%."
T: "Then where would you rank 'awful' on the same scale?"
K: "Over 100%!"
T: "Could it be that by using the term 'terrible,' you have added a frightening dimension to an event that was bad for you?"

M. Vlajkov, *Basics of Rational-Emotive Behavior Therapy*,
https://doi.org/10.1007/978-3-032-19448-0_19

K: "Yes, that's right. I can see that!"
The therapist has now completed the decatastrophizing process. He asks the client, "How do you feel that you have gained this insight?" The client answers: "It's not as bad as I imagined, I can live and cope with it."

Another way to test catastrophizing as an irrational thinking pattern is described below:

The therapist asks the client to rank various unpleasant events on a scale of 0%–100%. A "0" stands for an event that is neither disadvantageous nor unpleasant. An ultimately unpleasant and disadvantageous event is represented by a "100." If the client describes their own death as 100% unpleasant, then no event could be rated higher.

The client lists the worst possible events that are immediately below the 100% mark. The therapist then describes to the client even more severe events than those the client has given. When asked, "How do you classify these newly named events on a scale of 0–100%?" the client rates them as 100% catastrophic. The therapist then mentions much worse events and asks the client again how they rank them on the scale compared to the previously mentioned events. In this way, the client is forced to re-conceptualize his evaluation system. An example illustrates this procedure:

A client comes in for therapy. During the psycho-diagnostic interview, she stated that it is terrible for her to have to work four hours a day because she doesn't feel up to it. In the first therapeutic session, the therapist explains the catastrophe scale to her and asks her, "Where do you classify your situation on a 100% scale?" Her answer is: "100% bad!" The therapist replies that the classification of her situation seems very interesting to him. He gives her the following visualization exercise: "One morning, you are walking through the forest. You are on a narrow path near your house, at the edge of the forest. Suddenly, you see a cyclist coming towards you. You can't avoid him because there is a fence on one side of the path and a precipice on the other. The cyclist brakes, but the wheels skid on the soft forest soil. You realize that he is going to crash into you. Where is this situation on the 0–100% scale?" She says: "The absolute 100!" Now the therapist asks the crucial question: "How bad or severe is it for you to have to work four hours a day compared to the possibility of being run over head-on by a cyclist?." She reassesses her situation (having to work four hours) and downgrades it from 100% to 5%. The therapist goes one step further and describes the following situation to her: "Imagine you are on a cruise ship with 2999 other passengers. You have your own cabin, and the ship is approaching the coast of Ethiopia. Suddenly, you hear a voice over the ship's loudspeakers telling you that pirates have hijacked the ship. You are abducted from the ship and taken inland. Two large men tie you to a tree. These men sit on the ground next to you and begin eating. They talk to you in a language you do not understand, but you realize they are talking about you because they frequently look at you. You are tied tightly to the tree and cannot move without pain. You cannot go to the toilet, eat, or drink anything. You cannot sit down and are forced to stand all the time. The area is full of mosquitoes, and you have the impression that these mosquitoes have just been waiting for your blood. Large swarms of mosquitoes land on your skin and literally 'eat you up.' After a few minutes, your body begins to swell. How would you rate this situation on the 100% scale?" She responds: "Definitely 100%! It would be a disaster for me!" The therapist responds: "How bad are four hours of work a day?" The client: "It's good that I have a job and that I live in a safe society instead of being tied to a tree!" The therapist then asks: "What could you think about your work in an alternative way instead of continuing to be firmly convinced that it is terrible to have to work four hours a day?"

So, the rational alternative is: "I don't like working four hours a day and wish I didn't have to go to work, but compared to other inconveniences in life, it's harmless, of course." The last question in this therapeutic sequence is: "How do you feel when you think like this?" The client's answer is: "I feel uncomfortable, but I can still work."

In the second part of the therapy, the therapist discusses the functional aspects of the client's situation. In the example given, he would ask the client whether having a job is disadvantageous for her. The client's likely answer would be: "Basically, it's the best situation for me because otherwise, I would be unemployed, have less money, and therefore less personal freedom."

When clients gain insight through the described process that their situation is not as bad as they thought and sometimes even turns out to be "good," they realize that their idea of life was overly idealistic and unrealistic. Clients often compare their idealistic and unrealistic view of life with their life situation. Through this comparison, they evaluate their current situation as bad and disastrous. When clients shift their focus from the idealized view of life to the objective facts and possible alternatives, they free themselves from their inhibiting feelings and begin to look for better life options.

Through this process, clients recognize the following two possibilities:

1. Either they put up with their current living situation because there is no better alternative for them,
2. Or they find a way to change something about their situation so that they feel better.

Chapter 20
Global Rating and Challenging the Global Rating

The global rating occurs when you describe or label others, life situations, and yourself using nouns or adjectives. Examples of global ratings include:

- Calling a person who smells of garlic a "stinking pig."
- Calling a friend who is procrastinating on a joint project "lazy" or, even worse, "lazy pig."
- Calling a crashed computer "junk."
- Describing bad weather as "absolute filthy weather."
- Seeing yourself as a "failure."

Global ratings usually lead to a negative attitude towards oneself, others, objects, and circumstances.

In therapy, we often hear clients refer to other people as liars, cheaters, bullies, peasants, country bumpkins, lucky bastards, or heroes. If someone is labeled as stupid, insidious, a stubborn ass, a sly fox, a foolish dog, or a person who has been washed with all the water, this creates a global rating.

These expressions can cause emotional problems. If the therapist identifies an emotional blockade in a client who uses these expressions, they refer to this type of irrational thinking as a global rating.

When Albert Ellis developed REBT, he did not know how to question his patients' global ratings efficiently. He was inspired by the research contributions of the semantic linguistics expert Alfred Korzybski (1933) and applied a special procedure described below. In his research, Alfred Korzybski ascertained that all descriptions of states expressed with the verb "to be" ("He is a stubborn donkey!") should be replaced with descriptions of the concrete situation or action ("He behaved like a stubborn donkey in this situation!").

Martin Seligman laid the groundwork for positive psychology through his research on "learned helplessness." The German psychiatrist Nossrat Peseschkian (Peseschkian, 1985) developed positive psychotherapy based on this. Albert Ellis

M. Vlajkov, *Basics of Rational-Emotive Behavior Therapy*,
https://doi.org/10.1007/978-3-032-19448-0_20

created a procedure from Korzybski's approach and positive psychotherapy that allows for global rating to be checked efficiently. This is done as follows:

1. The therapist first identifies statements that express global ratings and elicit an unpleasant, unhealthy feeling.
2. Global ratings are usually derived from a person's behavior. The "labels" are then attributed to the person.

Examples: If a person tells a lie, they are lying. If the person is labeled a liar based on this fact, it constitutes a global rating. If one person yells at another and is labeled a choleric person, that is a global rating. If someone bumps into another person and doesn't apologize, labeling them a bully would be a global rating.
Suppose a client ascribes a characteristic to a person based on their behavior. In that case, the therapist asks the client: "How can a person's behavior in a certain situation determine the nature of that person?" For example, a father promises his son that he will buy him a new bicycle for his next birthday. The father breaks his promise, and his son gets angry and calls him a liar. In this situation, the therapist asks specifically: "Is it logical to think that an unfulfilled promise makes the father a liar?" "A liar" is someone who has always lied in the past, is lying in the present, and will always lie in the future because it is their nature (in other words, they could never tell the truth).

A second way to check global ratings is to use a metaphor. Most people are familiar with the Dalmatian dog breed. These dogs have black spots on a predominantly white coat. The therapist asks his client: "Is the Dalmatian white or black?" The client usually answers: "Mixed—both black and white!" The question follows this: "If someone has told the truth nine times and lied once, is this person a liar or an honest person? For example, if a father keeps his promises nine times and forgets once, is he a liar or a good father?" In this way, the therapist points out to his client that it would make more sense to describe the specific situation and behavior, rather than deriving a global rating from them.

Martin Seligman went one step further. He defined the process by which unpleasant, unhealthy feelings are replaced by pleasant feelings. These feelings relate to other people, life situations, and the individuals involved. Martin Seligman recommends not only describing positive events as positive but also evaluating them globally. For example, if a soccer team wins a game and the players not only claim to have played better but also claim to be better than the others, then this is a global rating. This creates an inflated sense of self-worth and self-respect.

Martin Seligman (Seligman, 1990) argues that most people have an innate tendency to explain everything that happens to them. He categorizes these explanatory models into two types: constructive or self-destructive. In an example about a soccer team, one explanatory model is that some players performed worse, and others won because of that. As a result, success is attributed to chance. Martin Seligman recommends that the winning team describe themselves as the "better" team, attributing their success to themselves.

Albert Ellis considers the explanatory model recommended by Seligman to be a hindrance to developing an objective attitude toward one's own reality. Such individuals become uncritical and self-satisfied about the facts they evaluate. From the REBT perspective, it is advisable to describe both pleasant and unpleasant events as they truly are. In this way, each person's adaptability is strengthened, and a remarkable resilience against emotional disturbances is built. This (objective, clear-minded) way of thinking means mobilizing all resources to solve any life situation. In this context, it can be said that it is not the most intelligent and beautiful who have the best lives, but those who adapt best to their circumstances!

Chapter 21
Low Frustration Tolerance and Challenging the Statements That Relate to It

This form of irrational belief is usually expressed as "I can't stand it!" or "I can't bear it!" However, the person who thinks this (or says it) is still enduring discomfort at that moment. Just by asking the client if they really can't stand it, the person becomes aware of the statement and weakens it by adding, "Well, maybe I could stand it. But just the mere thought of the unpleasant situation is almost unbearable for me." In this way, the client proves to himself that he can create a feeling of severity and nausea through his own thinking.

Albert Ellis introduced the idea of frustration tolerance into psychotherapy in the 1960s. At that time, Americans began to enjoy the full benefits of industrialization. Nearly every household had a car, refrigerator, vacuum cleaner, washing machine, dishwasher, electric food processor, coffee maker, and air conditioning. Additionally, anesthetics and painkillers were widely used for the first time, making surgeries practically painless and significantly reducing discomfort. The downside of this progress was that people were no longer exposed to life's inconveniences and saw any sudden discomfort as a personal catastrophe. Previously, dental procedures for cavities were extremely painful. With anesthetics, these treatments became almost painless and caused less discomfort. Industrialization and medical advances expanded people's "comfort zone." Today, this trend continues, and people live more comfortably, exerting less effort to satisfy their desires than in the past. Pizza delivery services bring food to your door quickly, the internet makes communication easier, and people no longer need face-to-face meetings to share their thoughts; they seem to learn less and retain less information. The decrease in both mental and physical effort lowers frustration tolerance, which can lead to psycho-pathological problems.

M. Vlajkov, *Basics of Rational-Emotive Behavior Therapy*,
https://doi.org/10.1007/978-3-032-19448-0_21

There are two forms of low frustration tolerance:

1. People are exposed to certain inconveniences that they should be able to tolerate. For example, if the hot water boiler suddenly breaks down and people can only use cold water temporarily, they should tolerate this inconvenience.
2. Choosing between two pleasant alternatives is often tricky. The person who has to make a decision frequently finds it unbearable to go without one of these options, so they delay the decision for as long as possible.

The therapist should ask everyone who claims they cannot bear something the question: "If you were to expose yourself to this unpleasantness, would you die from it?" When they realize they can endure and bear the unpleasantness, they increase their frustration tolerance.

How can this be curbed? How can someone disengage from the belief that they cannot bear something, and how can they stop avoiding unpleasant situations?

The low frustration tolerance is at the core of different forms of anxiety, especially *specific phobias*. The author of this book developed the treatment for specific phobias during an extended session in 1981. At that time, it consisted of two parts. He called the first part *cognitive restructuring* and the second part *exposure treatment*.

Cognitive restructuring involves the client becoming aware of the thought pattern that causes the fear of a specific object or situation. This thought pattern takes the form: "I can't stand it!" For therapeutic success, it is enough to replace this thought pattern with a new one, thereby motivating the client to face the discomfort they have avoided for years. The new thought pattern is: "Although it is difficult for me to endure this, I know that I can stand it!" An example of this is the fear of injections. The author of this book has treated several hundred people who were afraid of injections. These clients initially thought that the pain could increase endlessly and that they would either go mad or die from it. After saying the new thought out loud to themselves several times, they were ready to start the second part of the treatment: exposing themselves to the discomfort.

The success of this therapeutic intervention depends largely on the therapist's skill. Sometimes, the specific phobia is based on the client's conviction that he cannot tolerate his fear of discomfort. As a result, the client is condemned to live in an anxious state (discomfort anxiety). It is often the case that other irrational thought patterns precede this disorder. The client can only be cured if the therapist identifies all the thinking patterns that contribute to this disorder, examines them, and replaces them with rational thoughts.

Chapter 22
Formulation of Rational Alternatives

There are two approaches to formulating rational alternatives.

1. The therapist offers the client the rational alternative by formulating it himself.
2. The therapist asks the client several questions to help the client formulate the rational alternative himself.

The first approach is known as the didactic method, and the second as the Socratic method.

The didactic model is used in REBT only when the client needs instruction on specific issues. The therapeutic process basically involves a dialogue between the therapist and the patient.

The didactic model is usually used when the relationship between thinking and feeling needs to be explained to patients using an example. Patients should recognize the point of the example themselves.

Example: A patient is afraid of taking the elevator. In the first part of the therapy, the therapist explains to his patient that the elevator did not diREBTly cause the patient's anxiety, but rather the way he thinks about it. When the therapist asks his client what goes through his mind while he is in front of the elevator, the patient usually says he sees it as a dangerous place. Suppose the therapist asks further what is hazardous about an elevator. In that case, the patient answers that the elevator could get stuck between two floors and that he would remain trapped in the elevator until he suffocates. Such patients believe that an elevator is a metallically closed object from which there is no escape and into which no fresh air can enter. They think that they will quickly use up the oxygen in the elevator and that they will suffocate, like someone who has a plastic bag pulled over their head. If a therapist were to ask the same question to a person who is not afraid of the elevator, they would get the following answer: "I don't think about anything, I just go in and use it as a vehicle." When asked whether the elevator is dangerous, he replies that it is just as harmful as any other place in the world.

M. Vlajkov, *Basics of Rational-Emotive Behavior Therapy*,
https://doi.org/10.1007/978-3-032-19448-0_22

The problem with "fear of taking the elevator" and other objects does not lie in the client's relationship to these objects, but in the conviction that he could not stand this fear. He believes he would lose control in this situation. From his point of view, this would result in either a mental or a physical catastrophe. In the first case, the client thinks that he would go mad and end up in a "loony bin," and in the second case, he fears a heart attack or stroke. He is therefore convinced that he must avoid any form of excitement and anxiety, which leads to his avoidance behavior. People with an intense fear of specific objects or situations not only avoid these objects and situations, but also their surroundings. By simply being in proximity to these objects, they assume they could become upset and begin to look for the symptoms of distress in themselves. As in the saying "Seek and ye shall find," the patients also find the signs of the physical or emotional catastrophe that is coming their way.

When should the didactic method be used? Especially if the client takes notes of all the therapist's explanations during the session, or if the session is made available to the client as an audio recording, which they should listen to as a homework assignment, and write down the essential content.

The difference between the didactic and the Socratic approach is that in the Socratic approach, the client is involved in the dialogue to keep his attention at a high level—he is thus "forced" to actively participate in the therapeutic process. It can be observed that with the didactic approach, clients often leave diREBT communication after just two sentences from the therapist and wander off. They withdraw into themselves and begin to brood. Only those therapists who can convey their didactic explanations in an interesting, humorous way and frame them as stories can maintain their patients' attention throughout the session.

The Socratic method is so called because the therapist proceeds as Socrates once did in ancient Greece. Socrates was known for being unbeatable in argumentative debates with his opponents. He asked them questions so skillfully that they gradually realized from their own answers that he was right and they were wrong. Since Socrates was a "stage hog," he often defeated his opponents in public.

The REBT therapist follows the same process. He knows the therapy's outcome in advance and questions the client's irrational beliefs with him, guiding him through questions to help him abandon those beliefs and replace them with rational ones.

At the beginning of therapy, the client represents and defends his own irrational beliefs. However, the therapist knows that these beliefs are irrational and untenable. He also knows that he will guide the client in this dialogue toward a cognitive insight—provided, of course, that the client cooperates. Skillfully asked questions are the therapist's most important tool.

In this way, the client gains insight and overcomes their emotional disturbances. There are three "levels of insight" that the client can achieve during a therapeutic session:

1. Cognitive insight
2. Emotive insight
3. Behavioral insight

Cognitive insight refers to the relationship between the irrational belief and the emotional consequence, known as the B–C connection. The B–C connection is explained to the client at least twice during a session.

The first time, the B–C connection is explained at an abstract level, outlining the basis of this therapy and how it works. The second time, it is presented to the client using a neutral example. In the third explanation of the B–C connection, the therapist uses the client's specific emotional problem.

Therapists should also point out the B–C connection to their clients several times throughout therapy. As soon as they discover an irrational thinking pattern in their client's statements, they ask: "And if you think like that, how do you feel?" In this way, the therapist prevents their clients from associating the situation with the emotional blockade, because they realize that the thought (B) serves as the mediator between the situation (A) and the emotional problem (C).

Emotive insight occurs when the client's own rethinking puts them in a healthy state of mind.

Example: If the client suffers from a panic disorder, the irrational thought is usually "I can't stand being afraid of having a stroke." I can't bear to go mad and end up in the loony bin." After examining the thought, the client and the therapist reason that he would be able to bear it after all, even though it is hard for him. The rational thought in this case would be "I don't like it when I get scared of a mental breakdown again, but if I have this fear, I can endure it, even though it is hard for me."

During therapy, the patient is given the task of writing down the thought and then reading it out slowly. Immediately afterwards, the therapist asks the client how they feel when they think this way. The patient usually reports feeling a sense of relief, although he finds it difficult to bear.

In this case, the emotive insight was the feeling of relief after the rational alternative was verbalized.

Every irrational thinking pattern can be replaced with a rational thought, and that rational thought is the solution to the client's emotional problem.

Rational Alternatives to Absolutistic Demands

Flexible, fact-based, and logic-based preferential thoughts are an alternative to absolutistic demands. In the context of REBT, logic refers to consequent (i.e., consistent) thinking. The logical consistency of a thought is tested by asking the following question: "Does it automatically follow that just because you want or desire something, you absolutely must have it? Is it logical to think that just because you want something, it must come true?" A good example of this is when a person claims they could not go on living without their partner and therefore their partner must not leave them under any circumstances! However, there was a time before she met her partner, and it is undisputed that she probably led a good and happy life for the most part back then. It was only when she got together with her partner that she experienced heartache, jealousy, envy, anger, fear, and depression. During the time without a partner, her personal freedom was greater because she didn't have to consider her partner or conform to anyone else. The fact that she led a healthy life before she met her partner suggests that she would survive a separation rather than die from it.

The use of such examples is of great strategic importance in REBT because they reinforce the client's rational conviction. This is the decisive precondition for leading the client from cognitive to emotive insight.

Emotive insight refers to the therapeutic change that occurs during a single session. It can be achieved in two ways:

1. The emotional change, the transformation of the unpleasant, unhealthy feeling into an unpleasant, healthy feeling, only takes place after the client has understood and unconditionally accepted the rational alternative.
2. The patient achieves an emotional change when he performs his rational-emotive imagery exercise as homework (this technique was introduced into psychotherapy by Maxie Maultsby (Maultsby, 1990), Albert Ellis adapted it to the REBT model, and it is described in the chapter on homework assignments).

Rational Alternatives to Global Ratings

The rational alternative to a global rating is to describe the specific events or behaviors as they happened, without adding anything beyond that. Examples of this are:

- "The teacher is unfair." The rational alternative to this is: "The teacher has mistreated me in this situation."
- "This driver is a moron!." The rational alternative to this is: "This driver cut me off and therefore endangered me on the road."
- "My boss is an arrogant bastard!." The rational alternative to this is: "My boss behaved arrogantly towards me this morning."

Rational Alternatives to Catastrophizing

A rational alternative to catastrophizing is formulated through the precise description of events, other people, and us. "Something is terrible!" is replaced by "Something is very unpleasant, but not terrible or horrible!" Statements that express an exaggeration (too warm, too cold, too damp, too many people in one place, etc.) are rephrased as "It is very warm!," "It is very cold!," "It is very damp!" and "There are lots of people in this place!" If there really were "too many" people in one place, this would mean that not everyone present would have found a place to stand on the floor, but that they would have had to be piled up. When the word "too" is used with an adjective (e.g., too much, too hot, etc.), it means that the person who resorts to exaggeration believes that there is "more" of it than they can bear. This thought is paradoxical, as the person is still alive and thinks "they can't stand it." If someone thinks there are too many people in one place, they feel crowded, cramped, and stressed. However, if the person thinks in the same situation, that there are many people in this place, they feel more at ease.

Rational Alternative to Low Frustration Tolerance

"I can't bear something" is replaced by the statements "I can bear it even though I don't like it" or "I can bear it even though I find it difficult." In this way, the fear of discomfort is transformed into a willingness to tolerate this discomfort. As a result, the person becomes courageous instead of remaining fearful.

Strengthening Emotive Insight

To turn a cognitive insight into an emotive insight, the client must consolidate his rational conviction so that he begins to believe it. To do this, the therapist uses the same procedure he used to assess irrational thinking patterns. The therapist checks the rational alternatives according to the criteria of consistency (logic), usefulness, practicability, and agreement with the facts. If the rational alternatives have met all the test criteria, the patient will begin to believe the rational statement, even if the therapist has formulated and given it to him.

During a therapeutic process, patients reach cognitive insight more quickly than emotive insight. Most people find it difficult to renounce the fulfillment of their wishes. For patients to convert a cognitive insight into an emotive insight, they would have to abandon the fulfillment of their own wishes, as they equate those wishes with demands. This is precisely why the therapist formulates a rational belief (rational alternative) in such a way that a flexible wish is first expressed explicitly, because the wish contains the possibility of not being fulfilled. Then the facts are listed that speak against fulfilling the wish. Finally, the acceptance that neither the wish nor the demand must be fulfilled is expressed.

For the patient to transform their cognitive view into a true emotive insight, the therapist recommends that they even give up their wishes as if they had never had them, especially when the patient realizes that their wish cannot be fulfilled and that continuing to wait for it is harmful to them.

An unfulfillable wish can have a secondary benefit for the patient, especially if it increases the patient's motivation to pursue the goal they have set for themselves. In this case, we speak of the so-called instrumental value of a wish. The therapist should assess this together with the patient; in that case, it would be advisable to either give up the wish, which turned into an absolutistic demand, or to keep it even if it cannot be fulfilled.

When the author once gave a lecture on personal development, someone in the audience asked him whether the Dalai Lama should give up his wish for the autonomy of Tibet, as he would obviously not be able to fulfill this wish during his lifetime. The answer to this question was that this unfulfillable wish probably motivates the Dalai Lama and his compatriots to maintain the dream of liberation and the free practice of their own religion. Thus, the Dalai Lama's unfulfilled desire for Tibet's freedom has a particular instrumental value (motivation). The secondary goals include, for example, maintaining national identity, preserving religious beliefs, and maintaining hope for freedom. Another secondary gain can be described as "public relations" for the Tibetan people, as it helped the public become aware of Tibet's national problem. Most of the world's population sympathizes with the Tibetans and supports them in their efforts for freedom. This is precisely why the Dalai Lama needs to hold on to his unfulfillable wish, since China has not yet agreed to negotiate with him, nor partial autonomy, nor recognition of the Tibetan population as a separate nation, nor freedom of religion.

To reinforce an emotional insight, it is advisable to examine all forms of rational justification (consistency, feasibility, usefulness, congruence with the facts). The therapist thereby leaves open the possibility that the rational conviction may be challenged in the same way as the irrational one. For example, if someone claims that something is terrible, the therapist offers them the alternative that it is not terrible, but only very unpleasant. The therapist compares this event with other, even worse, events. In this way, the therapist questions the term terrible. He asks the client how he feels when he describes something as terrible versus viewing the same event as merely unpleasant. In this way, the patient realizes that he can only overcome the unhealthy feeling if he evaluates the event objectively. Suppose the client's emotional response changes because of the re-evaluation. In that case, this confirms that the re-evaluation is corREBT and rational, which is beneficial to the client.

By challenging their rational beliefs, patients enable themselves to apply this type of thinking to future events. This increases their own emotional resilience in even more difficult life situations.

During a therapy session, a client complained that it's terrible when her daughter slams her bedroom door at seven in the morning without consideration, disturbing the neighbors. The client fears the punitive looks from neighbors in the stairwell and a decline in neighborly relations. The therapist explains that in Germany, it is legal to make noise in your own home from seven in the morning until ten at night. Therefore, the client's claim that the noise from the doors is terrible is exaggerated. This exaggerated sense of consideration and the use of the word "terrible" fuel her fear of neighborly disapproval. This fear stems from a low frustration tolerance because she believes she cannot handle the "unpleasantness" of an encounter with her neighbors. This example highlights the connection between her thoughts of meeting her neighbors alone and her fear. Rephrasing her statement, "The slamming of the doors is terrible!" to "I find the slamming of the doors unpleasant, but it's not terrible, even if some neighbors might find it slightly disturbing," could help reduce her anxiety. All of this revolves around the idea that her daughter should not give the neighbors any reason to feel disturbed. According to REBT philosophy, each person is responsible for their own emotional disturbances. A loud door slam is not what bothers the neighbors; it is rather their belief that neighbors should not slam doors and should be considerate. Importantly, the neighbors have never complained about the door slamming.

According to Ellis, irrational beliefs—described as global ratings—are the most difficult to challenge and replace with rational alternatives. The reason for this is that patients find it difficult to accept someone who has committed an "evil" act. People tend to label a criminal as an evil person, implying that this person is not only evil but also has been evil in the past and will remain so forever. They overlook the possibility that someone has committed an evil act out of a spontaneous impulse or a momentary desire. Most people find it difficult to accept the fact that even someone who has frequently committed crimes is not an evil person. For this reason, the therapist recommends that patients evaluate and label only deeds or traits, rather than transfer them to the person. To strengthen this conviction in the patient, it must first be adequately formulated and then checked against all the criteria mentioned several times.

Example: Was Al Capone an evil person? The general opinion, especially in the press, is that he was an evil person because he was a mafia boss, had commissioned countless murders, and was convicted of tax evasion. From the point of view of a therapist practicing REBT, it is obvious that the claim that Al Capone was an evil person is not tenable. Al Capone did not treat everyone in an evil manner, especially not his family, associates, and his many wives. The rational belief is: "It is true that Al Capone committed many crimes. That is a fact. Although it would have been better if he had not committed these crimes, that does not mean that he was a bad person per se. The question to be examined is: Why didn't these misdeeds make him a bad person?" If the assertion contained in this question can be plausibly explained to the patient, then the patient will change his mind and free himself from the emotional distress caused by a global judgment. For anybody who can think clearly, it is evident that an act or a specific behavior cannot change the nature or essence of a person. For this purpose, it is advisable to use many metaphors. Does spending time in church make you a good person, and spending time in the favelas of Rio de Janeiro make you a bad one? Or is a person, as they are, neither good nor bad in themselves, regardless of the circumstances in which they find themselves? Only then is it explained to the patient that a human is a complex being and that a behavior, even if it is repeated a thousand times, doesn't change his nature. The human remains a human being.

The credibility of the rational belief can be increased, for example, by asking the following questions: If a person grunts like a pig, does that make them a pig? If they sing like a nightingale, does that make them a nightingale? The same principle could be used to ask whether a talking parrot becomes a human being or whether it remains a parrot. Does an actor who plays a criminal become a criminal because he has allegedly killed and committed criminal acts in the role?

It is evident that neither behavior constitutes human nature, nor does human nature result in behavior.

A global rating has several functions in human society. Some of these functions are useful; others are harmful, especially if they cause an unhealthy feeling. In this case, it is appropriate to challenge the global rating and replace it with a rational statement.

If someone has told an untruth once, you are usually not quick to call them a liar. However, if you find out that this person has already lied 28 times, you typically call them a liar. The meaning of this label serves an adaptive protective function for the person in a relationship with the "liar." They know they can no longer rely on the "liar" 's statements.

Suppose a person evaluates another individual globally and, therefore, suffers from an emotional blockade (anger, rage, hatred, etc.). In that case, they can free themselves from these blockades by replacing the global evaluation of the person with a description or assessment of their behavior.

The Transfer of Emotional Insight Into Behavioral Insight

In the ABC model of emotions, point C (the consequence) consists of two parts:

1. The emotion.
2. The behavior.

Emotions mainly influence behavior. If the feeling is unhealthy, the behavior becomes self-defeating or harmful to the individual. When a healthy one replaces an unhealthy feeling, a person can change their dysfunctional behavior into a functional one. However, this does not happen automatically because this person has never experienced the functional behavior when they were emotionally blocked. Therefore, this person still needs behavioral training. If someone has avoided public appearances because of stage fright, they will not become an excellent speaker or actor simply by overcoming it. They might still lack rhetorical skills and the ability to interpret social signals.

The last part of the therapy consists of enabling the client to behave confidently and successfully in life situations in which they have behaved inefficiently due to their emotional blockades. This indicates that for therapy to be successful, the therapist should also have sufficient competence in the areas of their client's life. For example, if the therapist himself suffers from an inhibiting stage fright, he cannot credibly help his clients.

Chapter 23
Homework Assignments

Homework assignments are a key feature of REBT.
These have several functions:

1. Practicing the new way of thinking that the patient has learned during the therapeutic session.
2. The consolidation of the therapeutic effects achieved.
3. Practicing efficient behavioral patterns.
4. Applying the newly acquired way of thinking to new situations.
5. Increasing self-efficacy through the consistent application of therapeutic instructions.
6. The transfer of acquired knowledge to everyday life.

Over the past 60 years, the following categories of homework assignments were designed as part of the REBT:

1. Cognitive.
2. Emotive.
3. Behavioral.
4. Complex.

None of the categories listed relates exclusively to the domain designated by this term. A cognitive homework task also contains a small emotional and behavioral component. An emotive task can only be solved if the cognitive and behavioral approach is practiced. A behavioral task consists not only of the recommended behavior, but also of the accompanying mindset and the appropriate emotional state.

Complex tasks correspond to the so-called formal exercises in sporting disciplines. These formal exercises are used to practice the processes involved in performing specific behavioral units in sports, making them automatic and thereby raising performance to a higher level. Complex tasks are extracted from the client's everyday life and relate to the domains in which the client has tried unsuccessfully

M. Vlajkov, *Basics of Rational-Emotive Behavior Therapy*,
https://doi.org/10.1007/978-3-032-19448-0_23

to do something up to this point. The complex homework assignments should significantly increase his competence.

There are homework assignments corresponding to each stage of the therapeutic process. This results in a second classification of homework assignments. The therapeutic process begins with the diagnosis of the patient's emotional problems. Therapeutic sessions follow this to get to know the patient and establish an appropriate therapeutic relationship (which should be diREBTive and aimed at solving the problems). This is followed by sessions in which the patient's emotional problems are addressed and solved. Finally, the functional thinking patterns are consolidated, and the patient returns to their everyday life. This enables them to lead a more satisfying life. The therapist assigns specific homework tasks to the patient for each stage of therapy:

1. *Diagnostic homework*: This helps the patient gather the facts on which the therapist can test their diagnostic hypothesis.
2. *Probatory homework*: The therapist assesses the client's capacities for the desired therapeutic change.
3. *Homework to consolidate the therapeutic effects achieved.*
4. *Therapeutic build-up homework*: This helps the patient develop skills for activities they have struggled with so far.

In the rest of this book, the homework assignments involving various therapeutic interventions are described first. Then, the homework tasks assigned to each specific therapeutic section are explained.

Cognitive Homework

1. Working with the table (an example of the table can be found in Appendix No. 2 at the end of the book), the client receives the table with prepared irrational beliefs on the left-hand side. This column is labeled B. The column to the right of B is labeled D. In column D, the client should check his irrational beliefs by applying the learned procedure from the therapeutic session at home. They will receive precise instructions from their therapist. If the patient is dealing with his absolutistic demands, he learns to apply the questions that help him check the usefulness, facts, feasibility, and consistency of his demands. If the cause of the client's emotional problems is a global rating, the therapist provides them with three levels of evaluation:

   The first level consists of naming the event as it was perceived. The second level is called generalization, and the third level is abstraction. The following example illustrates this: a car driver has "cut off" another driver when overtaking, thereby putting them in danger. The "cut" driver perceived this behavior as "bad driving" (first level). From this, he concludes that the driver is a bad driver (second level); some people conclude that all other drivers are bad (third level).

The review of a global assessment and its corREBTion should be carried out at all three levels. First, the question is asked: Are all drivers bad? Then comes the question of whether the driver who cut the other person off has become a bad driver as a result, and finally, whether the act (cutting the other person off) was a bad act, and from whose point of view? Thinking patterns discovered in the patient during therapy, such as catastrophizing, are checked by asking the following question: Is the event "terrible" or just "bad"? In this case, the therapist assumes that his patient has already become familiar with the meaning of the word "terrible." The word "terrible" contains the dimensions "bad" and "frightening." "Bad" refers to how the patient perceives and feels about the event. The "frightening" dimension arises from the patient's belief that the event itself could strike terror into their bones. If the patient has attributed a frightening effect to an event, they can take back that effect and thus free themselves from the fear of the event. In this case, the event is experienced as it is, and the patient develops a fact-based attitude towards their reality, freeing themselves from emotional blockades. The author of this book does not deny that there are also real catastrophes that provoke intense fear in those in such situations. A possible natural disaster, war, or famine is a real disaster, and if one tries to trivialize this disaster, then a discrepancy arises between the disaster and the evaluation of it. In positive psychology and positive thinking, it is suggested to the patient that every event has something meaningful (therefore good) in it. Since this way of thinking is called folk wisdom, some clients can become resistant to therapy by treating it as fact and defending their own way of thinking on this basis.

An interesting consideration relates to the consumption of intoxicants, including drugs, narcotics, nicotine, and alcohol. Although it has been proven many times that these substances have an apparent adverse effect on the cerebral cortex, partial positive effects on thinking or emotional stability are still used to justify them. Some political parties advocate the idea that freedom of expression should not be restricted. From this, it is then deduced that freedom of conduct (consumption behavior in relation to intoxicants) is also a private matter for everyone. However, suppose it is already known that the consumption of intoxicants clearly has health-threatening effects. In that case, the author of this book asks whether it would not be better to educate children about this in school, using scientific facts, rather than leaving it to the children. Otherwise, they will form their own opinions through digital media and other forms of advertising. Ultimately, only through their experience do they become addicted to these substances. If their health is ruined as a result, it is often not possible to reverse the damage.

In statements about low frustration tolerance, patients learn how to question it. Low frustration tolerance is expressed by the sentences "I can't stand it" or "I can't bear it." With the question: "Can you really not stand it? Would that kill you, or would you die from it?," the low frustration tolerance can be checked and increased.

2. Formulating rational alternatives: This homework can be given to the patient in two ways. The first possible homework task is for the patient to write down the

rational alternative that he formulated together with the therapist in the session, twenty times a day, precisely as it was formulated in therapy. He should bring his notes to the next session. The second option is to give the patient the homework assignment to reformulate the therapist's rational alternative to achieve the desired therapeutic effect. Only then should he write down this formulation twenty times a day until the next session. The rational alternative consists of three parts. In the first part, a wish is formulated, in the second, the facts, and in the third, the acceptance of what cannot be changed. An example of a rational alternative looks like this:

"I wish to pass my math exam, and I will do everything that depends on me to pass it. The fact is that I've already failed twice, and I don't know if I'll pass it the third time. So, I don't necessarily have to pass it next time either, although I wish I could!"

Emotive Homework Assignment

The rational emotive imagery exercise (REI): Maxie Maultsby introduced this exercise into psychotherapy, and Albert Ellis adapted it for REBT. The instructions for the exercise are: "Sit comfortably and relax. Close your eyes. Imagine that you are … (this describes the situation in which the emotional blockade arises). Put yourself in the situation and allow the feeling to come up … What do you feel now as you actively imagine being in this situation? Intensify this feeling, allow it to overwhelm you completely, and now, without changing anything in the imagination, free yourself from your distressing feeling and feel … (the alternative healthy feeling). When you've freed yourself from your stressful feelings, please open your eyes.

The therapist waits a few minutes, and if the patient does not open his eyes, he continues: "I know you can do it, just apply what we have already discussed in this session. As soon as you have freed yourself from the blocking feeling, please open your eyes.

After the patient has opened his eyes, the therapist asks him the following question: "How did you manage to free yourself from the burdening feeling? What were you thinking?" If the patient reports that he has accepted the imagined (difficult, hard, or unpleasant) situation and thus overcome the stressful feeling, the therapist gives him this imagination exercise as a new homework assignment. If the client

- has not followed the instructions or,
- has changed something in the imagery or,
- has left the imagery and,
- has digressed or,
- has concentrated on changing bodily sensations,

it may be that the distressing feeling has been alleviated. Although the therapeutic goal—to free oneself from the distressing, dysfunctional feeling—has not been fully achieved, the therapist should continue the dialogue in the following way:

"You did the exercise quite well and are now feeling better than before. However, there are even more elegant ways to free yourself from the stressful feeling." The therapist should then explain the ABC of feelings again and point out that the situation itself cannot diREBTly cause his feelings, but that his feelings are affected by how he thinks about it. By changing the imagined situation, the patient paradoxically reinforces his belief that the situation is causing his feelings. The therapist therefore recommends that the patient formulate a thought that will free him from his stressful feelings the next time he practices the imagery exercise.

It has been shown that some patients can use the imagery exercise more successfully than others. Those who cannot visualize a situation do not achieve sufficient therapeutic effects through the imagery exercise. Such patients should be given behavioral and cognitive homework. For those who can visualize, especially those who suffer from flashbacks, this exercise is an appropriate homework that can help them achieve the best therapeutic effect.

The author once treated a patient who had to travel to different European cities every day for work. He made these exhausting business trips in his car. After a few weeks, he realized that he could not endure this effort in the long run. All his colleagues in his industry flew from one place to another by plane, but he traveled hundreds of kilometers by car every day because he suffered from a fear of flying. When he first presented himself at the author's therapeutic practice, the author initially thought that he would not be able to free this patient of his fear of flying in just one session. Paradoxically, the session lasted less than an hour, and the patient reported that he was now ready to get on an airplane and fly. A week later, the patient contacted me by phone and reported that he had flown several times in the last week. He was also planning a long-distance trip to India with his family. He was then able to board the plane so calmly that he sometimes fell asleep in his seat before take-off. The therapy's success was due to the patient's ability to visualize the feared situation, which enabled him to free himself from the fear using cognitive restructuring. He realized that his rethinking helped him overcome the fear.

Behavioral Homework

1. Assertiveness training is an exercise that the therapist conducts with the patient during a therapy session. The therapist then assigns the same exercise as a homework task.

   How is this procedure carried out? First, the therapist uses the REBT model to determine which situations are problematic for the client. He then applies the "inference chaining" procedure to determine the thinking patterns underlying the problem. These thinking patterns are the cause of the patient's anxiety in the identified situations. After formulating rational alternatives to replace problematic thinking patterns, the patient practices applying them through an imagery exercise (REI). After overcoming the fear of the imagined situation, the patient is ready to be exposed to real situations. There are three categories of patients who face their problematic situations in different ways.

The first category of patients exposes themselves to the most challenging situation without hesitating or thinking about whether they can endure it. The second category of patients is those who think about how far they can go and are prepared to go to the limit. In the third category are patients who only want to face the discomfort gradually. Only after they have become accustomed to the slightest discomfort are they ready to move on. For these patients, the procedure known as "systemic desensitization" is most suitable. For patients in the first two categories, "flooding" or "exposure treatment" is used. The therapist assigns daily homework until the next session. On the first day, the client should complete a simple task, with each following day's task becoming gradually more challenging.

The rest of the chapter describes the basic exercises for overcoming the fear of public speaking, known as "social anxiety."

a. "Shopping exercise": The patient is advised to visit a shoe store and, if female, to find a pretty, young male sales assistant; if male, to approach a pretty, young female sales assistant. The patient should select the ugliest shoe model on display and ask for it, requesting a size at least two sizes larger than what would properly fit. After receiving the shoes, he puts them on, walks proudly around the store, then looks the sales clerk in the eye and asks if she likes the shoes on him. The usual response is: "The shoes look good on you, but aren't they a bit too big?" The patient usually does not expect such a reply, as they anticipate being laughed at and asked to leave. When told the shoes might be too big, the patient is instructed by the therapist to respond: "My brother has slightly bigger feet than I, so that we could share the shoes!"
b. "City center exercise": Anyone experiencing social anxiety is advised to go to the city center and ask the people there where most gather (either in the market square or in front of the town hall), where specifically they are. If the answer is: "You are in front of the town hall (or on the market square)," he should reply: "I'm not that stupid, I'm asking you which town I'm in!"
c. "Seduction exercise": Male patients who do not have the confidence to approach women they do not know are instructed to ask a young mother who is out for a stroll with her baby in a baby carriage for a "date." They should always look for a woman they like very much. The patient's goal is not to arrange a date, but to endure the highly probable rejection.
d. "Shame attacking exercise": People who fear public embarrassment or exposure should be tasked with dragging a leashed banana behind them in the pedestrian zone, like a dog. Occasionally, they should speak to the

banana with the following words: "Quiet! Sit! Sit! Could you give me your paw? Look at that pretty poodle watching you!"

e. "Beggar exercise": The therapist suggests that the patient dress in a stylish manner, wearing a suit with a white shirt and tie. They should stand in front of the church, extend their hand, and address the believers with these words: "I have neither father nor mother, I am all alone and poor. God will bless you, please give me alms! May your heart ache when you see me so miserable in front of you! I have nothing to eat or drink. Please give me a few dollars. Please! Please!"
f. "Pharmacy exercise": The patient should enter a busy pharmacy, filled with shoppers, stand at the end of the queue, and shout from there: "Please tell me if you have condoms here so that I know whether I should wait or go to the next pharmacy." If the answer is: "Yes, we have condoms!," he should then ask the following question: "Do you also have small condoms?" - the patient should expose themselves to the curious looks of everyone present and let the situation unfold. Another augmentation of this exercise is to ask the pharmacist the following question: "Do you have any chocolate-flavored or colored ones?." After giving this exercise to several patients, one of my last patients came up with a creative approach. Finally, after asking about the small condoms, he said, "I'm not buying them for myself, I'm buying them for my brother."

All the exercises above should be practiced until the person stays emotionally calm in the same situation and realizes that it is not the situation that is causing the discomfort, but their thoughts.

Diagnostic Homework

This homework is assigned to clients who come to therapy based on the recommendation of their family doctor or relatives. These clients are often unaware of their emotional issues and seek treatment with the hope of quickly resolving them. They also do not realize they are emotionally blocked until others point it out. For example, suppose a patient claims they are not suffering from any emotional issues and only started therapy because their dentist recommended it due to grinding their teeth at night. In that case, the therapist should explain the connection between involuntary and voluntary physical actions. If the patient understands that their nighttime teeth grinding is a natural response to emotional tension, they may be willing to try cognitive behavioral therapy. If a client can't recall a situation where they felt angry or frustrated but continued working, ignoring their emotions, the therapist might assign homework: keeping a diary of uncomfortable situations. This helps the patient become more aware of their emotional problems. Research shows that patients with bruxism and long-term alcoholics often first admit to emotional issues this way—these revelations can trigger a new emotional response, leading to irrational thoughts and further emotional and behavioral difficulties. However, a downside of this homework is that some patients start to obsess over bodily symptoms, becoming upset at the slightest physical reaction. The author advised patients not to overemphasize physical symptoms, but sometimes this caused them to notice even more and become more anxious.

One diagnostic homework assignment is called “self-monitoring.” It involves patients observing themselves and identifying signs of an emotional disorder. They should log which symptom they noticed, when they noticed it, and how they felt about it. Using this data, they attend the following therapeutic session to reconstruct the emotional blockage that caused the symptoms through a personal conversation with the therapist. The therapist explains to the patient how to recognize an emotional blockage when doing this type of homework assignment.

An emotional blockage manifests itself through:

- “Freezing” the mind.
- Slowed thinking.
- Hectic thinking.
- Chopped up thinking.
- Wrong thinking.
- Divergent thinking.
- Analog thinking.
- Misconception.

Emotional suffering manifests itself through:

- “Mental pain."
- The conviction that you can’t stand something.
- An urge to avoid or leave the situation, or to ingest chemical substances to alleviate the suffering.

Acute physical symptoms are another sign of emotional blockages:

- Palpitations.
- Sweating.
- Stomach cramps.
- Anesthesia in some parts of the body.
- Tingling in the face.
- Weakness in the legs.
- A feeling of confusion in the head.
- Be befuddled.
- General restlessness.
- Involuntary twitching in the muscles.
- The impression that the patient is on the verge of a physical catastrophe.

Psychosomatic disorders:

- Bruxism (night-time teeth grinding during sleep).
- Weak immunity.

- Asthma.
- Hormonal disorders.
- High blood pressure.
- Digestive disorders.
- Skin allergies.
- Food intolerances.

Inadequate motivation for the activity they are engaged in:

- Quantitatively insufficient motivation is demonstrated by the fact that people are either over- or under-motivated. Over-motivated individuals are tense and deplete their resources too quickly, preventing them from completing the activity they've started. Under-motivated individuals use their resources too sparingly, wasting time and failing to finish the task.

Qualitatively inadequate motivation is demonstrated by:

- The urge to please someone (whether an attachment figure or oneself),
- The pursuit of social recognition or high status and prestige.
- The expectation of a secondary gain (initially highly motivated, but a reactive depression develops when the expected benefit docs not materialize).
- The subdivision of motivation into the terms' extrinsic motivation and intrinsic motivation (whereby intrinsic motivation corresponds to adequate motivation, and extrinsic motivation is inadequate because it is or will be imposed from outside).

Preparatory Homework Assignments

This type of homework involves identifying the prerequisites needed to reach the therapeutic goal. It is mainly used with patients who struggle with procrastination. For example, suppose a client is delaying because he fears the discomfort of studying. In that case, he should stay in that situation and shift his emotional state to his advantage using the ABC of emotions. Only after he transitions to a healthier emotional state (anxious instead of fearful) should he organize his study area, so he feels motivated to learn. This organization includes having only the necessary documents on his desk and removing all other items from sight. This way, he trains himself to maintain focus and dedicate himself solely to the pursuit of learning. The prerequisite for this homework is that the therapist does not suffer from procrastination and is familiar with self-management and time management techniques. The therapist should be able to devise a more effective plan than the client could on his own. The essential first step in this process is to identify and address the underlying anxiety that causes procrastination. By taking these steps, the client prepares himself to handle his daily responsibilities.

Homework to Consolidate

The Therapeutic Effects Achieved

These homework tasks are complex and involve cognitive, emotional, and behavioral techniques. Two types of these tasks are presented below.

1. *"Empty chair" technique:* The client places an empty chair in front of him. He attributes his own irrational part to this empty chair. This part thinks irrationally, acts impulsively, and is obsessed with its own uncontrollable desires. The client should imagine a stressful situation for himself. He begins a dialogue with the empty chair. He himself plays the role of his rational being, and the empty chair represents his irrational part. This separation of the same person into the rational and irrational parts makes it easier for the client to apply the techniques he has learned during therapy to identify his own problems, review his irrational thought patterns, and replace them with rational beliefs. This technique can be combined with other techniques. The therapist gives the client additional instructions, such as asking the empty chair questions to check irrational thought patterns out loud. With the next instruction, the therapist asks the client to say the rational alternative even louder and to repeat it several times. The client should try to formulate the rational alternative as precisely as possible and ensure that this formulation is completed until it causes the emotional change. This procedure serves to strengthen the conviction in the rational alternatives and drown out the irrational part.
2. *Recording an inner dialogue between the client's rational and irrational parts, followed by listening and corREBTion,* is similar to the "empty chair" technique. The client records this dialogue, then listens and corREBTs any thinking errors and irrational thought patterns they identify. This process helps the client become more aware of irrational thinking and refine their rational responses. The goal is to rephrase irrational statements into rational alternatives that bring relief. A variation involves assigning the client the homework of collecting their irrational thoughts by writing them down or recording them during spontaneous, impulsive moments. This technique has proven especially helpful for depressed patients.
3. **"Stop technique"**: Patients who suffer from uncontrollable rumination are assigned this technique as homework. Before applying the stop technique at home, it must be practiced during the therapy session. To do this, the therapist follows this procedure:

   Please sit down comfortably, close your eyes, and imagine yourself in the same situation you were in the last time you cried. Let all your thoughts come up and tell me how you feel. If the client says they might cry again, the therapist continues with the following words: "Allow this feeling to overwhelm you! Feel deeply depressed and sad and keep ruminating."

   At this moment, the therapist should clap loudly and shout "Stop!" to interrupt the patient's rumination. When asked whether the therapist's loud shouting and hand clapping have disrupted the patient's rumination, patients usually respond "Yes." Next, the therapist should explain to the client: "Please repeat the same procedure on your own by shouting 'stop' loudly to yourself and clapping your hands." After the patient has completed the exercise, the therapist explains, "If you start to ruminate in a social situation, you obviously cannot use this technique out loud. Please repeat this procedure silently so that every time you catch yourself ruminating, you interrupt this rumination with a mental, silent 'Stop!'"

4. **Substitute activity***:* The patient should then make a list of meaningful activities. After applying the stop technique, the patient should pick an activity from this list and use it to replace ruminating. Each of these meaningful activities should meet the requirement that it captures the patient's attention in a way that prevents rumination when performed. Examples of such a list include writing an email, washing glassware, having a phone conversation with someone, or counting backwards from 500 to 1 at intervals of 7 or 13. After a few minutes, the mental "itch" (the author's term for the urge to ruminate) disappears. If the patient cannot interrupt the ruminating with the stop technique, then they suffer as much from their compulsive ruminating as someone who is forbidden to think about "little white elephants" for the next five minutes. In this case, the homework is supplemented by the person setting a time for "free" ruminating. This helps them interrupt their own mental "itch" and postpone it to the time they have set for their thoughts. The "recommended" time for unproductive rumination should be immediately before sleep. For 15 minutes, she should say aloud everything that comes to her mind, preferably recording it. Immediately afterward, she should spend the next 15 minutes corREBTing her thoughts and falling asleep with these rational thoughts. The thoughts she has immediately before falling asleep are consolidated during sleep and transferred from short-term to long-term memory.

Irrational thoughts that happen during rumination aren't easily recognizable because they are expressed in a concealed form. Some hidden irrational beliefs are mentioned here:

- "If only I could get rid of the sweets!"
- "How could she do this to me?"
- Where on earth has she hidden my car keys?
- Why didn't she invite me to the movies?

By using this technique, the patient is made aware of thought patterns that contribute to his learned helplessness. Through rational reformulations, he releases himself from this helplessness. The phrase "If only I could free myself from sweets!" expresses not only the patient's desire to live without sweets but also an absolutistic demand that he must free himself from sweets under all circumstances.

If the patient asks himself during his ruminating, "How could she do this to me?" "Where did she put my car keys?" or "Why didn't she invite me to the movies?" these questions express not only the patient's pure curiosity, but above all his absolutistic demands. The question "How could she do that to me … ?" contains the absolutistic demand that she shouldn't have done it to him. The question "Where did she put my car keys?" contains two absolutistic demands: "She should have told me where the key is!" and "She shouldn't have misplaced the key!" The question, "Why didn't she invite me to the movies?" is not a neutral, curious question; as the brooding person is not really interested in why he wasn't invited, but by asking this question, he expresses his absolutistic demand and reproach that she should have invited him to the movies.

Once the patient can recognize their irrational beliefs in such questions and statements, they have taken an important step in therapy. Most patients quickly learn to examine their irrational beliefs and replace them with rational ones; however, they often find it difficult to recognize these beliefs because they are usually expressed covertly, leading them to believe they are not engaging in irrational thinking.

Chapter 24
Euphemisms and Dysphemisms

Euphemisms and dysphemisms are two subtle forms of irrational thinking, classified as "rhetorical figures," and are socially accepted. A euphemism can soften the description of a person, group, object, or fact. Conversely, dysphemism aims to devalue people, things, or circumstances, giving them negative connotations.

There are two groups of patients for whom euphemisms and dysphemisms are particularly common. The first group includes patients who grew up in a highly repressive family environment and have accepted a submissive role in social hierarchy. The second group consists of those raised in families with traditional values. In these families, reference is often made to the family's origins, and children learn the family history of several generations as if this would increase their own worth. In both groups, there are educational practices that often prevent children from expressing themselves freely. The children are not allowed to use morally unacceptable words, and what is considered morally unacceptable is defined by family standards. Additionally, these children must avoid other social environments seen as morally corrupt. Not all children from these backgrounds develop irrational thinking patterns, but the likelihood of developing irrational beliefs is significantly higher than for others (Gilovich et al., 2023). Therefore, it is crucial for therapists to identify typical activating events for these social groups so they can intervene appropriately with these patients.

M. Vlajkov, *Basics of Rational-Emotive Behavior Therapy*,
https://doi.org/10.1007/978-3-032-19448-0_24

Chapter 25
Further Therapeutic Work

The goal of further therapy with the patient is to sustain the long-term benefits achieved. Additionally, the patient is supported in acquiring skills they have not yet been able to learn due to emotional barriers. During ongoing therapy, the therapist should help the patient plan a future life scenario and establish long-term goals that guide their current life situation.

The author has discovered that patients who have developed a life vision can use it as a guide on their path forward. In this case, the life vision serves as a corREBTive to assess current activities and determine whether they align with it. If current activities are leading the patient away from their life vision, they should be replaced with purposeful, meaningful activities. There are several methods for developing a life vision.

The first option encourages the patient to imagine holding a magic wand that can instantly fulfill their wishes or help them reach their goals. The patient should consider what they want to change in their life and what they hope to accomplish. As a next step in developing a life vision, they write a letter to themselves, asking and answering three questions within that letter.

1. What does he want his children to say about him after he's gone?
2. What would his best friend remember after he passed away?
3. What should his fellow human beings be proud of that they had him as a friend?

The life vision developed this way is not only rich in content but also acts as a moral compass in the patient's life. When patients are assigned this task, they start to see their future through their personal values rather than short-term successes or current (dis)satisfaction. People hold different values. Those who align their lives with pragmatic values tend to pursue activities that benefit themselves. Those who emphasize aesthetic values, for example, see themselves as future great artists who

M. Vlajkov, *Basics of Rational-Emotive Behavior Therapy*,
https://doi.org/10.1007/978-3-032-19448-0_25

will enrich their era through their art. People guided by ethical values mainly aim to improve the quality of life for others and to help those in need, such as the sick, the poor, or those requiring education. This therapeutic approach consists of two stages.

1. Recognizing and overcoming the patient's emotional blockages.
2. Enabling the patient to lead a successful and fulfilling life.

If the therapist also considers the patient's continued personal growth, their therapeutic role becomes complete.

One of the key questions many therapists consider during their careers is whether they should model what they "preach" to their patients in therapy. For example, can a therapist with low impulse control effectively help patients who face the same challenge? Can anxious therapists successfully treat their own anxious patients?

Based on his extensive therapeutic experience, the author of this book claims that therapists who have themselves experienced and overcome emotional blockages are better equipped to understand their patients and possess a wider range of techniques for overcoming such blockages than those who have only learned therapeutic skills but have never applied them to their own lives. A therapist who has never struggled with an anxiety disorder is likely to see their patient's anxiety as a personal weakness and may therefore devalue the patient. Similarly, therapists who have faced several depressive crises and managed to overcome them using a cognitive approach tend to treat their depressed patients with more understanding and compassion than those who have never experienced depression. However, this does not mean that every therapist must have experienced all emotional disorders to help their patients effectively. Rather, they should primarily understand how emotional problems develop and how they can be resolved. This understanding enables the therapist to appear competent and supportive, rather than pitying the patient. "Sympathizing" with patients—that is, becoming depressed or anxious like them—is not the goal. Instead, understanding the patient's suffering means the therapist observes how these struggles originate and how they can be alleviated, without adopting the patient's emotional state. Such a therapist serves as a role model of emotional health that the patient can trust.

The author therefore recommends that all therapists in training quickly overcome their emotional blocks so they can leave a competent impression on their patients. In a therapeutic session, what the therapist does is more important than how they do it. Depending on the therapist's skills, the therapy will be effective. For example, if the therapist tries to solve the patient's problem in an unhelpful way by empathizing with the patient's emotional state, the patient's condition is likely to worsen at the start of the session. Then, once the patient can no longer deteriorate, there may be temporary relief. Some therapists exploit this by lacking knowledge about the development and treatment of emotional disorders. They tell their patients that feeling worse first is necessary before feeling better. They credit the therapeutic results to their own skill. However, the patient is so drained by suffering that this exhaustion temporarily blocks out irrational beliefs to reduce suffering in the short term.

Control Meetings

Once the therapeutic process is complete, the therapist arranges a follow-up session with the patient. During this control session, the therapist checks whether the therapeutic effects achieved are short- or long-term. It often happens that patients neglect the homework assignment recommended to them and relapse as a result. As relapses are to be expected, the first control session is arranged 14 days after the end of therapy. If it turns out that the patient has relapsed, a new therapeutic plan is agreed upon with the patient and implemented. If the patient has not relapsed, a new control session is held one month later. If the patient has relapsed in the meantime, the therapeutic process is started again; otherwise, a new control session is held three months later. The author recommends that the therapist remain in contact with his patients even after the therapy and the first three control sessions have been completed, and arrange further control sessions with them at three-month intervals. The aim of these control sessions is not only to check the patient's emotional state, but above all to teach them the skills they need to live a more successful and fulfilling life.

Further Support

For therapists to continue successfully accompanying their patients on the path of personal development, they must acquire knowledge and skills that extend beyond therapeutic skills. These include communication skills, self- and time management, creativity techniques, and the basics of healthy eating and physical exercise. The author recommends that all therapists practice regular cardio training to serve as role models for their patients. This includes running, cycling, swimming, and walking. In addition, the therapist should also practice stretching exercises (yoga, Pilates, or similar) consistently and regularly. The sports that most promote the body are the so-called team sports (soccer, handball, volleyball, basketball, etc.). However, they all have one shortcoming: the person who wants to practice them depends on the presence of the other team members.

The crucial aspect of personal development is meditation. An article on the promotion of brain functions was published in the English magazine "Newsweek" on January 10, 2011. In a meta-study that examined several hundred empirical studies, the author of this article found that three activities promote brain function the most:

1. Walking, at least three times a week, for a duration of 45 minutes.
2. Meditation.
3. Complex computer games—but only computer games in which sensorimotor functions, memory, and fluid intelligence are used simultaneously.

All other activities, known as "brain jogging," only promote the skills that are necessary for carrying out the respective activity. If someone trains their memory, they will only improve their memory; if someone trains their sensorimotor skills, they will only enhance these skills, but the learning effect will not be transferred to other brain functions. In fact, transfer occurs only when the activity someone is performing forces newly created brain cells to participate in that activity. Every day, the human brain produces between 500 and 2000 new neurons in the brain stem. These neurons push their way out of the brain stem into the hippocampus. They can only persist in the brain for longer than two weeks if they are used. If they are not integrated into existing networks, they shrink and disappear. It has been found that meditation is the only activity that simultaneously activates all cells of cortex. This keeps the cortex in an optimal state throughout life. The author therefore recommends that all therapists train themselves to meditate with their patients.

A special type of control session is held with those patients who have suffered from specific phobias. Specific phobias can be treated and overcome in a more extended session. This session lasts between three and four hours. The second therapeutic session is both a control session and the conclusion of the therapy. For all other emotional disorders, the control sessions do not have the status of a therapeutic conclusion but serve to prevent relapses.

Chapter 26
One-Session Treatment

This method was independently developed by Lars Göran Öst, Thompson E. Davis III, and Thomas H. Ollendick (Öst, Davis III, & Ollendick, 2012), as well as the author of this book. The point of Lars Göran Öst's method is gradual behavioral change through exposure to the situation, whereas the author of this book achieves therapeutic change through cognitive restructuring during exposure.

The following describes the author's process, which he completed on his travels in Latin America. At the pyramids in Yucatan (Coba, Chichen-Itza, Uxmal), he was confronted with the panic-stricken fear of those who climbed the pyramids, stayed there, and then no longer dared to descend. These people sat with their backs against the pyramid wall, shaking with fear and drenched in sweat. In the 1980s and 1990s, it was common practice to "rescue" tourists with a fear of heights from the pyramid platform by helicopter. As a result, the tourist association issued a ban on tourists climbing the pyramids at the beginning of the twenty-first century. One of the steepest pyramids is the Pyramid of Chichen-Itza. In the middle of the pyramid wall is a steep staircase with extremely narrow and high steps. A steel chain hangs down from the top, which you can hold on to as you ascend and descend.

Some tourists only realize how high and steep the pyramid is, and the "danger" they have put themselves in, once they reach the top. When the author of this book first arrived at the platform of this pyramid, he found more than 20 people there, in a state of shock, sweating, and panicked under the Yucatan sun. Someone had "called" a helicopter, and they were waiting to be rescued. The author approached them and promised to guide them down from the platform so they could walk without fear, like "tightrope walkers." Of course, none of those present initially believed the author, but their curiosity was piqued. The author didn't wait for their consent and continued speaking because he had been practicing hypnotherapy for years and knew he needed to capture their attention. He asked those who could get up from the floor.

M. Vlajkov, *Basics of Rational-Emotive Behavior Therapy*,
https://doi.org/10.1007/978-3-032-19448-0_26

Some people stood up; others stayed seated. To those seated, the author told them to lift themselves slightly off the floor then sit back down. He repeated this several times with the seated tourists, and after a while, he asked them to crouch down. They all followed his instructions. He asked how they felt. They said they were scared out of their minds. Next, he asked what they were thinking, and they all said they thought they might fall off the pyramid and that they should stay seated. He then asked when they could better control their balance—standing or walking. They all said: "When walking!" The author told them to check this by comparing how they felt when walking versus standing. First, they all stood up, then crouched down again because they dared not stand fully. He suggested they stand up and take a step forward, then back, and then forward again. After a few repetitions, he told them to take two steps forward, two back, and after a few moments, two forward and just one back. Everyone realized they could better control their balance when moving forward and back than when standing still. When they realized that moving forward provided more security, some of them began carefully descending the stairs.

The core of this therapeutic approach is to keep the patient in a state of optimal tension. The therapist should make progress quickly in the therapy. The therapist promises not to do anything against the patient's will, but to leave the choice to the patient. The therapist uses techniques known in hypnotherapy as trance induction methods. Additionally, knowledge from social psychology is used to influence others (Cialdini, 2018). The author already had experience influencing others well before, having treated patients with hypnotherapy for over 40 years and trained hundreds of therapists in the practice. To get a person into a hypnotic trance, it is necessary to capture the patient's attention so they are not distracted and can only focus on the hypnotist's suggestions. In the situation described above, the author knew he needed to capture the tourists' attention so they would not be distracted as they descended from the pyramid. Over 20 years, the author repeated and refined this technique with patients and established rules that can help any therapist successfully treat a specific phobia in just one session. The rules are as follows:

1. Act as an expert.
2. Show expert skills.
3. Expect surprises and uncontrolled patient behavior.
4. Never give up on achieving the therapeutic goal in the therapeutic session (never give up).
5. Continuously cognitively restructure the beliefs associated with each specific situation.
6. Identify the irrational thought pattern and replace it with a rational one, then apply it to each specific activating event.
7. Whenever an emotional block occurs, identify the irrational belief behind it and highlight the B–C connection.
8. The therapist should be able to demonstrate each therapeutic technique to the patient in person. For example, if the patient fears needles, the therapist should prick themselves with a syringe; if the patient fears spiders, the therapist should be able to let a large spider crawl over their hands.

9. Every 10–15 minutes, the therapist should take short breaks to summarize what has been achieved so far and clarify what remains to be done. Two irrational thought patterns are consistently monitored during this process. The first pattern relates to the client's low frustration tolerance and is expressed by the statement "I can't stand it!" The second pattern is catastrophizing, as shown by "It's terrible!" Once the patient begins to automatically replace these two thought patterns with rational beliefs, he is prepared to confront the critical situations ahead.
10. The therapist should become familiar with all aspects of the patient's situation and feel confident about it. Additionally, they should be able to tolerate any discomfort they wish to expose their patients to, demonstrating that it is manageable.

The author once had his friend's daughter as a patient. She suffered from a fear of heights. After a therapy session, they went to a location about 20 km outside Stuttgart where the patient could be exposed to heights. This was a fortress built on a hill, with a deep abyss. To reach the fortress, you had to climb a few hundred steps up the hill. From there, you could look out over the Neckar Valley with its vineyards. The weather was sunny on the way up, but when they reached the top, it suddenly changed. Fog rolled in, and it drizzled. The therapist demonstrated the exposure exercise to the patient. He climbed onto the outer wall of the fortress and balanced about 4 meters on the edge of the vertical precipice. He was able to save himself at any time with a small jump back to the inside of the wall. When the client told her parents what she had done during the therapy session, they were so frightened that they said they would never have allowed her to participate in this therapy if they had known what danger she would be exposed to. The client replied: "That was the best thing that could have happened to me in my life! I've become brave and am no longer so cowardly and fearful." This patient went on to study psychology and became a specialist in treating anxiety disorders.

In "one session treatment," the client is assigned homework to confront the situations they fear until they have solidified the therapeutic gains. This homework should be done continuously for at least four weeks. It should also be explained to the client that the fears may return if they stop occasionally exposing themselves to these critical situations. Most psychotherapists face relapses from their patients. Especially after completing psychotherapy, it is common for patients to start experiencing the problems that had previously been addressed.

Why Do Relapses Happen After Completing Therapy?

1. Ivan Petrovich Pavlov, a Nobel Prize winner in physiology or medicine, is famous for discovering conditioned learning. However, he received his Nobel Prize for his research on the salivary glands of frogs and dogs. Pavlov also contributed to clinical psychology by observing the "spontaneous recovery of an extinguished reaction" in his experiments. In his studies, Pavlov noticed that his

dogs began to "drool" as soon as he approached them in the kennel. He wondered why the dogs were drooling and concluded they were doing so because he was feeding them. He then designed an experiment to demonstrate conditioned learning. Right before feeding the dogs, he rang a loud bell and repeated this up to 40 times. As a result, the dogs began to drool at the sound of the bell. He described the dogs' reaction as a "conditional" response and the bell's sound as a "conditioned" stimulus. Later, he wanted to "extinguish" the dogs' conditioned reaction, which he did by stopping the feedings after the bell rang. Over the next few months, he observed another phenomenon that happened by chance. The dogs, which had shown no reaction to the bell's sound for months, suddenly started drooling again at the unexpected sound. He called this the "spontaneous renewal of an extinguished reaction." The author of this book observed a similar phenomenon in his patients, especially those suffering from anxiety disorders.

The author's theory states that a reaction cannot be "deleted" but can only be "replaced" by another reaction. In the range of possible reactions to the same stimulus, both old, supposedly deleted, reactions and new reactions are stored in the brain. When the brain's activation level drops, the supposedly deleted reaction reappears and remains under control only when the person raises the "alertness level" in the brain. Only then can the person consciously use the newly learned reaction.

2. Impulse control: This homework is assigned to clients who have difficulty controlling their impulsive behavior. People who often become very angry and quickly lose control are asked to use an alarm signal to help them stop their aggressive behavior. This signal can act as a warning to "bite their tongue" before yelling at their children or acting out aggressively. It might also involve pressing their thumb against the fingernail of their index finger until it hurts, serving as a distraction from their anger. This homework should be practiced consistently for at least two weeks. Ideally, the client should replace irrational thoughts with rational ones immediately after activating the alarm signal, which can help reduce their inner tension. It is important to explain to the client that once inner turmoil begins, it will last for at least 15 minutes, as the body takes that long to lower stress hormone levels. However, this only works if the client consistently applies rational thinking. If they get unnecessarily angry about the automatic biological stress response, the stress reduction process may be extended by an additional 15 minutes.

Part 3
Errors in Psychotherapy

Chapter 27
Errors in the Psychotherapy

Psychotherapy relies on various approaches. Different therapeutic schools focus on other aspects of the psychotherapeutic process. Therefore, it is hard to pinpoint general errors in psychotherapy. Common errors across schools usually stem from not following the ethical code of conduct for all psychotherapists. In this chapter, the author will only describe errors relevant to rational-emotive and cognitive-behavioral therapy.

These errors can be classified as follows:

1. Errors resulting from the inadequate application of the theoretical approach.
2. Errors resulting from the inadequate application of the structured procedure in psychotherapy.
3. Errors stem from the inconsistent application of learning principles.
4. Errors caused by the misinterpretation of patients' answers.
5. Errors are caused by inadequate knowledge and inadequate therapeutic skills on the part of the therapist.
6. Errors resulting from the inadequate therapeutic relationship between the therapist and the client.
7. Errors caused by the therapist's active resistance to the patient's beliefs (conflict with the patient).

M. Vlajkov, *Basics of Rational-Emotive Behavior Therapy*,
https://doi.org/10.1007/978-3-032-19448-0_27

Chapter 28
Incorrebt Application of the Theory-Driven Approach

The theory-driven approach within the framework of REBT is based on the model that emotional disorders are caused mainly by the patient's thinking. Emotional disturbances can arise from the patient's past, but the patient's current thinking can explain their maintenance. Nevertheless, it is common for a rational-emotive behavioral therapist to adopt their patient's idea and accept the claim that the patient is suffering because his circumstances are unfavorable, or his peers are "unpalatable" to him. If the therapist begins to corREBT these circumstances or the behavior of others to reduce their patient's suffering, the therapist has replaced a constructive therapeutic approach with a "comforting" approach. This type of therapy prevents the patient from gaining insight into the relationship between thinking and feeling and reinforces his irrational thought patterns. Up to this point, the patient has thought that his fellow human beings and his life circumstances are responsible for his suffering, and now he is strengthened in his conviction by this therapeutic error.

The misapplication of the theory-guided approach can be avoided if the therapist constantly reminds the patient during the therapeutic session that the unhealthy feeling is caused by the patient's thinking. Each time the patient associates the activating events with the unhealthy feeling, the therapist should intervene by explaining to the patient that it is not the events but his thinking about the events that is causing his emotional disturbance.

If, during the therapeutic session, the therapist and the patient consider the activating event as the cause of the patient's suffering, then they contradict the core principle of the cognitive approach, which states:

It's not the things themselves, but how we see them that causes human suffering.

A second error from incorREBTly applying the theory-driven approach occurs when the therapist begins using so-called palliative techniques, such as relaxation methods, breathing exercises, various physical activities, avoidance behaviors, distractions, and more. These techniques aim to lessen the patient's feeling that

M. Vlajkov, *Basics of Rational-Emotive Behavior Therapy*,
https://doi.org/10.1007/978-3-032-19448-0_28

something is "unbearable" and to reduce their physical restlessness. This often leads the patient to believe that, on the one hand, the feeling is "unbearable," and, on the other, that their circumstances are responsible for it. Recognizing this error is especially important in a type of therapy called "one session treatment," which is used for specific phobias. It involves exposing the patient to the activating event after they have cognitively processed the cause of the disorder. When the patient is exposed to the activating event, muscle tension naturally arises. This tension should not be relieved through relaxation or palliative techniques, as it helps the patient adapt to the situation. Overall, it can be concluded that the therapist can only properly implement the theory-driven approach by consistently applying the B–C connection and guiding the patient to understand this relationship, enabling them to control their own feelings.

Conclusion: On the one hand, errors arise when the theory-driven approach is applied exclusively to the activating events (A) at the expense of the patient's irrational beliefs (B), and on the other hand, when the therapist tries to help the patient through palliative techniques.

IncorREBT Application of the Structured Procedure in Psychotherapy

Rational-Emotive Behavioral Therapy is a precisely structured process that includes specific stages within each session. These stages have already been described earlier in the book. At this point, the author will explain what happens when some of these structured steps are skipped or not followed in the proper order.

Error Regarding the Activating Events

An incomplete description of the activating event (A) results in an inaccurate formulation of the patient's irrational belief (B). Since the core of therapeutic change is based on the identification, verification, and reformulation of irrational beliefs, it is obvious that the irrational belief can only be formulated precisely if the object to which it refers is accurately described. This also leads to the conclusion that the therapeutic effects can only be fully achieved if the activating events are adequately and precisely described. The author therefore recommends that all therapists pay sufficient attention to the activating events of their patients, as this is the only way to precisely identify the irrational beliefs.

The second mistake in relation to the activating events occurs when the therapist begins to focus exclusively on these events and thereby reinforces the irrational beliefs of his patients. Even if the excessive preoccupation with the activating events does not solidify them, the therapist loses a substantial part of their time, and both the therapist and the patient become exhausted. This exhaustion has a paradoxical effect on the patient. If the therapist and their patient stop dealing with these activating events without having solved the patient's initial problem, they both feel as if they have run a "marathon." The patient has the impression that he is feeling better, not because he has solved his problem, but because he has given up or interrupted the search for the solution.

The solution to both above errors is for the therapist to devote sufficient, but not excessive, attention to the description of the activating events.

How can the therapist determine whether they have grasped the activating event and whether the patient has described it sufficiently? If the therapist has understood the patient's activating event, he can easily recognize the thought pattern underlying the emotional disturbance using the "inference changing" method.

Errors Regarding Unhealthy Feelings

The first error of this type occurs when the therapist does not identify the clinically relevant problem but instead begins to address the problem the patient states. This error occurs due to inadequate psychodiagnostics examination before the start of therapy. Another possible mistake is the therapist's lack of knowledge about the distinction between healthy and unhealthy feelings.

Suppose the therapist cannot explain to the patient why they should replace an unpleasant, unhealthy feeling with an unpleasant, healthy feeling. In that case, the patient might set an unrealistic therapy goal—assuming they will feel comfortable and relaxed in the same situation where they have been feeling distressed. If the therapist accepts this goal, they are likely to fail during the session because the situation for which the patient seeks treatment is at least unpleasant, if not threatening. In such cases, the patient cannot be expected to feel comfortable and relaxed on any given day. For example, if a patient fears having a painful tooth treated and claims the treatment will be unbearably painful, their therapist will ask how they would like to feel in this situation. Patients usually answer that they want to feel comfortable and relaxed. If the therapist agrees to this goal or wish, the patient will likely be very disappointed, as dental treatments are probably never completely pleasant.

What is the solution to patients' unrealistic expectations? The therapist should explain to the patient that a healthy feeling can also be unpleasant because of the circumstances the patient finds themselves in. If the patient accepts that they are replacing their unhealthy, unpleasant feelings with new, healthy feelings, they will develop trust in their therapist, as this goal can be easily achieved in a therapeutic session.

Another error related to emotions occurs when the therapist fails to recognize the complexity of the patient's emotional disorder and treats it simply as a problem. Examples include depression and generalized anxiety disorder. Both are clinically significant issues and represent a syndrome of specific emotional blockages. If the therapist does not address these disorders strategically, he may end up "going around in circles" with the patient and be unable to help because each of these clinical pictures is based on several irrational beliefs.

What does a problem-solving approach look like in these cases? The therapist should analyze each clinically relevant problem and identify the specific emotional blockages involved. In the second step, each of these issues should be treated as a separate problem.

Inadequate Explanation of the B–C Connection

Even if the therapist explains to his patient that it is not the events themselves that have caused his suffering, and the patient understands this in an instant, he may quickly forget it again, as if he had never heard of it.

If the therapist thinks, "I have already explained it to him once and he should have understood," the therapist will focus solely on their demand that the patient remember it. The therapist will overlook the chance to check what is missing in the patient's understanding of the B–C connection.

As mentioned earlier in the book, there are two levels of knowledge of the B–C connection.

- The specific level.
- The abstract level.

If the patient hasn't understood the B–C connection on either the concrete or abstract level, and the therapist expects the patient to have understood it long ago, the patient leaves the session convinced that external events are the cause of his suffering. This deepens his irrational beliefs instead of challenging them. Only when the patient realizes that his own thoughts are responsible for his suffering and his recovery is he willing to adopt the new way of thinking permanently and apply it in all critical situations in the future.

How can the therapist avoid this error? This consists of two stages:

1. The therapist should pay careful attention to the patient's statements and quickly determine whether the patient has understood the B–C connection. If not, the therapist can first explain the B–C connection using several examples, helping the patient understand it on a concrete level. They should then work with the patient to understand it on an abstract level.
2. In the second stage, the therapist uses the "role play" technique. The therapist takes on the role of the patient and portrays the patient's irrational belief. The patient should examine this irrational belief and replace it with a rational alternative from the therapist's perspective.

Errors in Relation to the Therapy Goals

The author has conducted several thousand supervisions of his students who have received specialized training as psychotherapists. In these supervisions, he discovered that the most common mistake in the therapeutic process is that therapists often fail to formulate a goal for the therapeutic session with their patients. This invariably results in patients not knowing why they should examine their irrational beliefs and what the purpose of a rational alternative is. Even if they have understood the B–C connection without having formulated the goal of the therapeutic session, the patient lacks the motivation to actively participate in the therapeutic process. This results in an inappropriate relationship between the therapist and their patient because the patient gets the impression that the therapist is trying to persuade them to do something instead of seeing the therapist as a source of therapeutic change.

Another mistake happens when the therapist agrees with the patient's wish to feel "comfortable and relaxed" in a tough situation. For example, if a patient has stage fright (fear of speaking in front of others) and says they want to feel relaxed and comfortable during a public performance, even under everyone's eyes, the therapist should not support this goal. It's unrealistic for the patient at this point. Instead, the therapist should set a new, more achievable goal for the session. This goal could be for the patient to feel less uncomfortable in public and only a little worried about how others judge them, without feeling fear. The patient might sweat or have tense muscles, but if they are free of anxiety and in control, they've reached their therapy goal. In short, the therapist needs to check if the patient's goal is realistic and step in if it's not.

Another mistake occurs in the therapeutic process if the therapist accepts that the patient's goal is too low. This can lead to the emotional problem not only remaining unresolved but also becoming worse and more ingrained. An example is a patient with a fear of heights. Overcoming this fear involves two key steps. First, the fear is reduced cognitively through a structured therapy session. Second, the patient is exposed to heights. If, during the second phase of therapy, the patient only expresses a desire to descend from a height once, the therapist should not accept this as the goal. Instead, they should agree on a more challenging objective with the client. The therapist suggests that the patient should aim not only to conquer the height once but also to put themselves in the situation multiple times in a row. Additionally, the therapist advises the patient to move fairly quickly to help maintain their balance more easily. The goal is for the patient to continue practicing until they have not only defeated their fear but are also able to enjoy it.

An experienced therapist understands that anxious patients often have reduced sensorimotor control and feel insecure in critical situations. Suppose these patients can significantly improve their sensorimotor control and maintain perfect physical balance during an extended therapeutic session. In that case, they will experience a strong sense of achievement and feel as if they have overcome their emotional blockades. This not only provides them with inner satisfaction but also sparks enthusiasm for reaching this important goal. The emotional aspect of therapeutic success strengthens the newly developed mindset and indicates that emotional conditioning has occurred.

Errors Regarding the Choice of Clinically Relevant Problems

During a therapy session, the therapist first identifies the patient's primary emotional issue. If he fails to consider a possible secondary emotional problem, he may struggle to address the primary issue effectively. It has already been explained that the secondary emotional problem can hinder the patient from resolving the primary one. Additionally, the patient might even have a tertiary emotional problem. For this reason, the therapist should always assess all levels of any emotional problems present and then decide which should be addressed first (primary, secondary, or tertiary).

Example: During a panic attack, the primary emotional issue is the fear of large open spaces because the patient believes they will lose their balance, fall, and sustain serious injuries. The secondary emotional issue occurs when the patient begins to constantly monitor themselves, checking if everything is okay with their balance. If they notice any bodily sensations they interpret as signs of imbalance, fear arises that they may no longer be able to control their balance. The tertiary emotional problem develops if the patient fears experiencing some unpleasant physical sensation at any point. This specific fear should be addressed first. If the therapist does not identify and treat one of these issues, these panic attacks may happen again after therapy ends.

False Identification of Irrational Beliefs

These errors can be grouped into two categories. The first is when the therapist misinterprets the patient's statements. The second is when the patient's deductions are viewed as irrational thought patterns. If an irrational belief isn't corREBTly identified, then a valid rational alternative can't be formulated from it. For example, when the patient says, "I have to accept my boss's criticism," the therapist might interpret this as an absolutistic demand from the patient, rather than recognizing a low frustration tolerance in the statement. This could be rephrased as "I can't stand my boss's criticism!" The rational alternative for this misunderstood thought pattern would be: "I wish I could accept my boss's criticism. If I don't accept it, then I don't have to!" For low frustration tolerance, the rational alternative might be: "I find it difficult to put up with my boss's criticism. But the truth is, I have tolerated it so far, and I will likely tolerate it even more easily in the future!" Of these two, only the second alternative will bring relief and help the patient deal more constructively with his boss in the future.

Accepting inferences as irrational beliefs is a common mistake in therapy. It typically happens when the therapist does not fully execute the "inference changing" technique. When the therapist reviews the inference with the patient and replaces it with a more accurate thought, the patient is likely to experience temporary relief. However, the emotional block will remain because the core of the emotional issue has not yet been addressed. The solution is for the therapist to consistently apply the inference-chaining technique until the true underlying thought pattern is identified.

IncorREBT and Insufficient Formulation of Rational Beliefs

The most common mistake in forming rational beliefs happens when the patient refuses to accept facts that conflict with their absolutist demand. Patients often create their rational alternatives using the word "can" instead of "may" or "doesn't have to." For example, if a patient claims that his child should clean up the playroom before 8 p.m. but does not, the patient faces the reality that contradicts his claim. He demands that his child tidy up the toys, but the toys are still scattered on the floor.

How can the patient overcome his anger toward the child? At the therapist's request, the patient formulates a rational alternative: "It would be nice if my child would tidy up his toys by 8 p.m. But the fact is that the toys are not tidied up by 8 p.m. That's why they can keep lying around." If the therapist agrees to this "rational alternative," he would reinforce the patient's irrational belief and, consequently, his anger toward his child. The outcome would be a therapy failure.

How can this mistake be avoided or corREBTed? First, the patient's genuine desire is expressed. The fact that argues against fulfilling the wish is stated, and finally, this fact is accepted—with the statement "it may be as it is" and not "it can be as it is," because this "can" is far too gentle for true acceptance.

The Error of Inadequate Application of Beliefs

A proper formulation of the rational alternative alone is not enough to create lasting therapeutic change. Especially if the patient is not yet convinced of the validity of this rational alternative, the emotional insight gained can diminish over time, and the disorder may relapse. Therefore, therapists also review rational alternatives with their patients. Different techniques are employed to strengthen these alternatives. In the example above, the patient may not be convinced that toys can be left out after 8 p.m.; in this case, the patient needs to demonstrate to the therapist why leaving toys out after 8 p.m. is acceptable. If the therapist does not find the patient's arguments credible, they should challenge the patient's statements.

Errors in the Dispute

The dispute is a process for examining both irrational and rational beliefs of the patient. Therapeutic success can only occur if the patient recognizes that his irrational belief is causing his emotional problem. This irrational conviction should then undergo a systematic review because only through this review can a rational alternative be formulated. The error in therapy occurs when the therapist fails to check the irrational belief against all relevant criteria. These criteria are:

1. Consistency
2. Usefulness
3. Consistency with the facts
4. Feasibility

Another error in the dispute occurs when the therapist fails to apply the criteria mentioned earlier to examine rational alternatives. Since the patient is usually not convinced by the rational alternative because it includes a part he dislikes, the therapist is advised to teach him that the part he dislikes is also valid. This part, which the patient rejects, is expressed through statements such as "it may be as it is" or "it does not have to be as he wishes it to be." The shift from a cognitive to an emotional insight happens only when the patient not only recognizes the truth of the rational alternative but also believes it.

Errors in Relation to Homework

The first error of this kind occurs when the therapist assigns a homework task that isn't suitable for creating therapeutic change. For instance, a patient has just learned in therapy how to come up with rational alternatives and is given the inappropriate homework to practice "REI" every day. Instead, the therapist should have assigned him the homework of writing it down 10–20 times a day to reinforce the rational alternative he just learned. An additional instruction for this task is not only to write the rational alternative in a standard way, but also to consider how it can be rephrased to maximize the therapeutic benefit for the patient.

The second error occurs when the therapist fails to give instructions on positive and negative reinforcement for completed or incomplete homework. This can lead the patient to sabotage themselves, skipping homework or doing it irregularly.

The therapist makes another error when he accepts his patient's statement that he doesn't need homework because he has understood everything. The result is limited therapeutic progress and inadequate application of this progress in the patient's daily life.

The final issue related to homework occurs when the patient begins randomly changing the assignments given by the therapist. For example, a patient with social anxiety might be tasked with confronting more difficult social situations each day.

If the first task is to ask passersby for the time, the next should be to inquire about their location. For instance, if they receive an answer:

"You are in the marketplace!" Then he should ask: "In which town?" Some patients avoid jumping to the next, more difficult level and stick with the first, easier homework task.

Errors Related to the Control Sessions

Three types of errors can be identified at this stage. The first occurs when the therapist fails to schedule any control sessions. The second happens if the control session is scheduled either too early or too late. The third relates to the content of the control sessions.

A control session mainly involves evaluating the patient's emotional state and how effectively he has applied the cognitive approach to his emotional issues. If the therapist uses the control session only to assess the patient's emotional state without offering corREBTive or therapeutic intervention, the patient might think everything is fine and that he doesn't need to change anything.

For example, patients often start replacing the cognitive approach with positive thinking. If the therapist does not respond with proper cues and challenges to the patient's positive thinking, the patient is likely to continue this distorted way of thinking. This can lead to relapse.

Chapter 29
Errors Arising from the Inconsistent Application of the Learning Principles

Three learning principles are essential for the cognitive approach:

1. Instrumental learning
2. Insight learning
3. Model learning

The therapist applies the principle of instrumental learning if, for example, he uses positive and negative reinforcement to ensure that homework is completed. It is crucial to emphasize that the therapist should use partial rather than systematic reinforcement, as only partial reinforcement ensures long-term therapeutic change.

Suppose the therapist only describes and explains the B–C connection to the patient without encouraging him to gain insight through questions. In that case, this is an incorREBT way to apply insight learning. If the patient does not seek insight on their own, the learning process slows, and therapy lasts longer. This was confirmed in an experiment with rats. Two groups of rats had to learn to navigate a maze. Each time the rats reached the end and ate the food, they were returned to the start. This process was repeated until all the rats learned the way to the goal. The rats were divided into two groups from the start. Each rat in the first group had to pull a small cart behind it. The rats in the second group had to pull carts loaded with heavy stones. It turned out that the second group learned the way to the goal twice as fast as the first group.

In the famous Hawthorne experiment, conducted between 1928 and 1945 by Elton Mayo (Gillespie, 1991) and colleagues, it was discovered that test subjects working under more challenging conditions performed significantly better than those in ideal conditions. In this task, participants had to screw small parts together. The workplace was brightly lit for the test subjects. The experimenters then gradually decreased the lighting for half of the participants each day. Toward the end of the study, half of the participants worked by candlelight and still performed better than those working under ideal lighting.

M. Vlajkov, *Basics of Rational-Emotive Behavior Therapy*,
https://doi.org/10.1007/978-3-032-19448-0_29

If a therapist applies these findings to insight learning, then after asking a question about the B-C connection, they should patiently wait for the patient's insight and corREBT answer. If the answer is accurate, the therapist should affirm it. If not, the therapist should find a "drop of truth" in the incorREBT answer and add the appropriate corREBTion. For example, if a patient fears suffocating in an elevator, the therapist might suggest riding in a Pater Noster elevator with no doors. The patient might accept this, realizing they cannot suffocate, or they might fear getting stuck between floors and suffocating. How should the therapist respond? How can they find a "drop of truth" in this response? The therapist could say, "I like the fact that you are telling me your fears so honestly. They assume that it is probably unrealistic. They assume that if the elevator gets stuck between two floors, it can be fully sealed. To do this, the floor between the two floors would have to be at least two meters thick. What do you think?"

The error in applying model learning occurs when a therapist works with patients who want to quit smoking or drinking but the therapist engages in those same habits himself. This makes the therapist untrustworthy in the eyes of these patients. For instance, an overweight patient seeks help from a therapist to lose weight. The therapist emphasizes the importance of healthy eating habits but drinks Coca-Cola himself. The patient may experience cognitive dissonance because the therapist isn't practicing what he preaches. To prevent this, it is recommended that therapists first apply the cognitive approach to themselves and "fix"[22] their own behaviors. Only after they can confidently lead by example will they be able to build trust and credibility with their patients.

Chapter 30
Errors Due to Misunderstanding Patients' Answers

These errors are difficult to classify because the therapist can misunderstand their patient in many ways. Whether the therapist will understand their patient corREBTly depends on the following factors:

1. The context in which something was said,
2. from the clinical picture of the patient,
3. The therapist's knowledge of the domain in which the patient's emotional problem occurs.

If the patient comes from a cultural background unfamiliar to the therapist, misunderstandings are more likely than in other situations. For example, if a Japanese patient tells a German therapist about feeling disgusted when seeing Europeans stick a fork or chopsticks into rice while eating, the therapist can only understand if they know that the chopsticks stuck in rice symbolize saying farewell to the deceased.

A therapist should understand their patient's clinical picture. If they do not, they might misinterpret their patient's behavior. For example, suppose a patient asks their therapist whether they can check what is behind the cupboard in the treatment room. In that case, the therapist might see this as a sign of obsessive-compulsive disorder or paranoia. However, if the question stems from a specific phobia (such as arachnophobia), then the therapist would not be providing appropriate help and would be applying the wrong therapeutic approach.

The following example highlights an error that occurs because the therapist lacks knowledge of his patient's field: The patient works at a nuclear power plant, where one of his duties is to monitor turbine pressure through digital displays. He panics about missing a potential pressure increase in time. If the therapist doesn't know whether this mistake could lead to a catastrophic event, like a turbine explosion, or just damage the brass instrument, he won't understand the true nature of his patient's fear. But if he knows that multiple safety measures are in place to prevent the turbine from exploding, he can have a factual discussion with his patient and help ease his fears.

M. Vlajkov, *Basics of Rational-Emotive Behavior Therapy*,
https://doi.org/10.1007/978-3-032-19448-0_30

Chapter 31
Errors Due to Inadequate Knowledge and Lack of Therapeutic Skill

Therapists who use the cognitive approach poorly and lack knowledge of learning psychology and psychopathology risk making errors. The REBT approach appears logical and simple at first glance. Many therapists think it is enough to apply this method without extra knowledge or experience. However, when faced with their own failures, they often believe they should continue using the REBT model rather than learning new skills to help their patients better. For example, a borderline patient might outsmart an experienced therapist by skillfully changing the subject during a session, preventing a proper collaborative relationship. A patient with narcissistic personality disorder constantly seeks admiration from the therapist. If the therapist attempts to show the irrationality of the patient's beliefs, the patient will likely devalue the therapist and see them as the enemy, interpreting this as a personal attack. A patient with OCD deeply believes they cannot think or act differently. Consequently, they are often unwilling to examine their obsessive thoughts. This resistance can be addressed if the therapist views the patient's obsessive thoughts and behaviors as activating events.

If the therapist lacks the necessary skills for certain stages of the therapeutic process, an anxious patient might notice these insecurities and assume that the therapist is incompetent. Such patients may withdraw from therapy and develop mistrust toward the therapist. To avoid this, it is advisable for the therapist to thoroughly practice each stage of therapy to project confidence to the patient. The therapist should ensure they do not just "work through" the therapy out of habit but remain aware of each therapeutic intervention, making every decision intentionally.

M. Vlajkov, *Basics of Rational-Emotive Behavior Therapy*,
https://doi.org/10.1007/978-3-032-19448-0_31

Faulty Therapeutic Relationship

The first mistake of this kind happens when the therapist tries to please their patient to build a positive therapeutic relationship. REBT does not involve the therapist providing emotional support to help the patient. Therefore, the therapist's attempt to please the patient conflicts with the core principles of the cognitive approach. This can cause the patient to expect positive emotional reinforcement in every session. However, if this reinforcement doesn't occur, the patient might feel abandoned, rejected, and unloved.

Therapists using the REBT approach are advised to establish a professional relationship with their patients where roles are clearly defined. The therapist has the knowledge and skills to address the patient's problems, while the patient is most familiar with their own. Humorously, it can be said that the therapist is an expert in problem-solving, and their patient is an expert in creating their own problems. Therefore, the patient's problems can be addressed effectively through collaboration.

The emotional relationship between the therapist and his patient is secondary or even completely unimportant for solving the problem. The therapist should only recognize if he himself has a desire to please his patient. If so, he should suggest that the patient see another therapist.

Another mistake in therapy happens when the therapist responds to the patient's unwanted behavior with an insult. For example, suppose the patient promises to complete the therapeutic homework but does not follow through. In that case, the therapist might feel offended, as he sees it as a sign of disrespect for his authority. In such cases, the therapist is not suitable to continue the therapy. This issue can only be fixed if the therapist first deals with his own emotional blockages.

Conflict with the Patient

During therapy sessions, unskilled therapists often try to persuade their patients to be more rational. They pressure patients to see the irrationality of their beliefs and to accept rational alternatives. When the patient resists this pressure, the therapist typically increases their efforts and insists that the patient adopt their viewpoint. This often leads to greater resistance from the patient toward the therapist's ideas. As a result, a conflict arises where the patient expresses their negative attitude with statements like "Yes, but … "

This error is rooted in logical reasoning because the therapist believes he is right and that his patient is wrong. He assumes that the patient must agree with him. Some therapists even become loud and insist that their patients repeat rational statements multiple times. They claim that repeating these rational statements during a session helps the patient gain insight. However, this approach does not align with the philosophy of the cognitive approach, which emphasizes a cooperative relationship.

Therefore, it is recommended that the therapist continually monitor their relationship with the patient. If he senses any resistance from the patient, he should address it by saying: "The patient has not come to me because he is insightful per se, but because he has not yet gained insight into the root of his emotional disorder. That's why he needs my help!"

Chapter 32
Termination of Therapy

The primary goal of psychotherapy is to help the patient resolve their own emotional blockages and disorders independently. Some patients lack the resources to learn all the self-help techniques, so the therapeutic process must continue with control sessions for these individuals. Sometimes, patients do not want to end therapy even after they have become capable of solving their emotional problems. In such cases, the therapist should not reinforce the patient's dependence but instead confront the patient with separation anxiety as the final issue and address it in two stages. First, the problem should be processed cognitively. Then, the therapist exposes the patient to separation and leaves "the door open" if the patient cannot "endure" it. If the patient seeks contact again, this is considered a new, clinically relevant problem.

The therapeutic process is sometimes ended at the patient's explicit request. It often happens that both the therapist and the patient conclude that the therapy is over at the same time.

In REBT, there is a limited amount of information and skills that patients should learn during therapy. Practicing self-help techniques and skills may take more time, but teaching the basic concepts of the cognitive approach and addressing the patient's immediate problems can be accomplished in just a few sessions (up to 10). If the therapist decides to end the therapy with the patient, he should tell the patient the following in the last session:

1. He lists all the therapeutic successes for his patient from the beginning to the end of the therapy.
2. He confirms to his patient that he has learned and practiced all skills and self-help techniques.
3. He explains to the patient that continuing the therapy would be immoral, as outsiders could interpret a continuation of the therapy as greed on the part of the therapist.
4. The therapist recommends books and articles that he considers helpful for the patient's further path.

M. Vlajkov, *Basics of Rational-Emotive Behavior Therapy*,
https://doi.org/10.1007/978-3-032-19448-0_32

Chapter 33
Strategy and Tactics of Therapeutic Work

The strategy of therapeutic work is based on basic postulates that the therapist relies on in rational-emotive-behavioral therapy. These basic postulates are as follows:

1. The ABC model of emotions.
2. Identification and verification of irrational beliefs.
3. Formulation of rational alternatives and their verification.
4. Consolidation of rational alternatives.
5. Application of rational thought patterns to the patient's life situations.

Each of the postulates listed can be further subdivided. This process of subdivision is the tactic of therapeutic work.

The therapist makes a strategic decision about when to transition from one level of therapy to the next. For example, the therapist determines when the patient should apply the insights gained in therapy to everyday life and test them out. Strategy involves abstraction, while tactics focus on how or by what means this abstraction can be accomplished.

Strategic progress in therapy occurs when the therapist recognizes the right moment to shift to a higher level of abstraction with the patient. The very first step in therapy is addressing the patient's specific, concrete problem. When this problem is not only resolved but also leads to the development of a new, rational thought pattern, the conditions are met for advancing to the next level of abstraction. This level involves applying general principles to solve the concrete problem. The highest level of abstraction is reached when multiple specific problems are solved consecutively, enabling the patient to handle all future critical situations using this strategy automatically. Whether the highest level has been achieved is indicated when the patient no longer needs to consciously think about problem-solving tactics, as they can spontaneously derive all necessary steps from the overall strategy.

In the author's opinion, this strategy has proven to be particularly important in the treatment of personality disorders and depression.

M. Vlajkov, *Basics of Rational-Emotive Behavior Therapy*,
https://doi.org/10.1007/978-3-032-19448-0_33

An example to explain the strategic approach in psychotherapy.

Reactive depression consists of several relevant clinical problems:

- Helplessness and hopelessness
- Despair
- Lack of drive
- Feelings of guilt
- Offenses
- Powerless rage
- States of anxiety
- Procrastination and avoidance behavior
- Various physical complaints (headaches, back pain, chronic fatigue)
- Loss of appetite
- Insomnia and so on.

Each of the listed problems should be treated as a separate, clinically relevant issue. If, during therapy, it becomes clear that certain thought patterns recur and are used to solve various problems, the therapist and the patient move to the next level of therapy. This stage involves creating a typical thought pattern from the individual thought patterns. From this typical pattern, a general pattern develops that the patient recognizes as applicable for eliminating all their psychological disorders, past, present, and potentially future.

Another strategic approach is based on the sequence of tasks assigned to the patient. Cognitive homework should be given first, followed by emotional tasks, and finally behavioral homework.

In treating anxiety disorders, an important strategic choice is whether the therapist starts with systematic desensitization as the initial behavioral homework or immediately exposes the patient to the feared situations, known as "flooding." This decision depends on the therapist's skill in assessing which approach best suits the specific case. "Flooding" is used only with patients who have expressed a willingness during therapy to confront difficult situations and endure discomfort. In contrast, systematic desensitization is typically used with those who leave a cautious, anxious impression on the therapist.

The treatment of psychotic patients and patients with personality disorders requires a special strategic approach. This strategic approach consists of the therapist viewing all symptoms in these patients as activating events rather than trying to change them. The patient will naturally expect the therapist to alleviate or eliminate their symptoms. For example, suppose the symptoms are hallucinations or persecutory delusions. In that case, the therapist should regard them as activating events (A) and not fall into the patient's "trap" because he would then try to verify the reality of the stated symptoms, which is not possible at all with psychotic patients.

The tactic always answers the question of how to carry out a strategic task. Tactics consist of several procedures that help the therapist choose the best way to execute strategic functions for each patient. The more tactical refinements the therapist knows, the easier it will be to make progress in therapy.

Chapter 34
Humor in Psychotherapy

What Is the Purpose of Humor in Therapy?

The therapeutic process is a serious matter in the context of REBT because the therapist expects the patient to participate actively, with a high level of concentration, to grasp the basic concepts of the cognitive approach, and to apply them to their own problems.

According to learning psychology, new skills are more effectively learned when the learner's emotional states support them. Although both pleasant and unpleasant emotions can boost learning, it is advisable to avoid the unpleasant emotional states as reinforcement. Humor helps make the patient feel comfortable during therapy. This underpins the positive reinforcement of the therapeutic effects achieved.

How Can Humor Be Used in Therapy?

There are various ways of presenting the relevant facts humorously and interestingly. These are:

1. Jokes and anecdotes that clarify insights; the therapist should continually increase their communicative competence by acquiring anecdotes from diverse cultural contexts.
2. Use of verbal contrasts, exaggerations, and paradoxical intentions.
3. Anticipation of various consequences of irrational thinking.
4. Exaggerations in the process of decatastrophizing.

For a therapist to use humor effectively in therapy, they need a certain sensitivity to it. If they lack this sensitivity and, for example, are the last to laugh at a joke, then they shouldn't use humor as a therapeutic tool. Only those who genuinely feel the

M. Vlajkov, *Basics of Rational-Emotive Behavior Therapy*,
https://doi.org/10.1007/978-3-032-19448-0_34

urge to laugh at different things and can spontaneously see the humor in situations are suitable to incorporate humor into psychotherapy.

The author witnessed an impressive example of humor in psychotherapy a few years ago while working with a patient who had conflicts with her mother-in-law. The mother-in-law was constantly nagging her daughter-in-law. They lived in the same house and depended on each other. When the author asked the client what the mother-in-law's intentions were in criticizing her, the client responded that she believed the mother-in-law acted with the best of intentions. The author then suggested that the patient imagine her mother-in-law as a mother hen surrounded by her chicks. When asked what the mother hen does to keep her chicks together, she replied: "The mother hen clucks!" "And what does your mother-in-law do?" the author asked. The patient burst out laughing and said: "She clucks too!"

At that moment, a strong therapeutic relationship was built between the therapist and his patient, and she was eager to follow all the therapist's instructions and complete all the homework.

Chapter 35
Forms of Therapeutic Work

Individual therapy sessions are the most essential form of REBT. It is not recommended for two people involved in a conflict to attend therapy together. The therapist is more interested in the emotional dynamics within the relationship and the feelings that hinder conflict resolution than in the relationship itself. The presence of others can only slow down and complicate the therapeutic process. From a cognitive perspective, emotional issues are often viewed as individual problems. Therefore, there are no shared emotional problems between two or more individuals. If a common issue exists, it is primarily a behavioral problem—how people interact with each other. Consequently, patients with interpersonal conflicts or relationship issues who attend individual therapy are often advised to switch to group therapy after some time so that they can address their behavioral problems.

This type of REBT is group therapy. It offers several advantages over individual treatment. The costs are much lower than one-on-one sessions, without reducing therapeutic effectiveness. The group setting helps address issues that may not be fully solvable in individual therapy, such as social anxiety, shame, or lumbosacral pain. Additionally, group therapy improves the therapist's efficiency, as each participant works on an emotional issue during the session, benefiting everyone. The group size is limited to 12 members, and sessions last 2.5 hours with a short break, giving each person the opportunity to focus on their emotional or behavioral challenges. People who disrupt the group or lack social skills are excluded from participation. Usually, two therapists—a main therapist and a co-therapist—lead the session.

A special type of group work is called a "therapeutic marathon." In this marathon, the therapist's job is to keep everyone's attention high and engage all participants so that everyone feels part of the process and stays involved for several hours. The therapeutic marathon is like a very long therapy session that

M. Vlajkov, *Basics of Rational-Emotive Behavior Therapy*,
https://doi.org/10.1007/978-3-032-19448-0_35

continues until all participants' issues are addressed. Both group therapy and the marathon draw on the group's resources to effectively handle participants' practical behavioral problems. The therapist is solely responsible for solving emotional issues during all group sessions. At the start of group therapy and the marathon, the therapist sets the rules for group work. The final rule is that anyone who breaks the rules must leave the group.

Part 4
Practice of Rebt

Chapter 36
Opening an Independent Therapeutic Practice

Once a therapist has completed their specialist training in psychotherapy and opened their own practice, they cannot expect immediate success or a large patient base. In recent years, competition among psychotherapists has become much fiercer. As a result, "young" psychotherapists rarely open their own practice, preferring instead to be employed by hospitals or existing practices. Despite all the adversity, some still try repeatedly. Faced with low patient demand, however, they often give up and leave their opportunities to work as an independent psychotherapist unused.

If someone wants to open a psychotherapy practice, they should follow these instructions:

1. The therapist should have sufficient competence and be aware that this competence enables them to help anyone who turns to them.
2. He should have built up an appropriate social network so that he quickly becomes known to as many people as possible and is recognized as a therapist.
3. He should have real practice rooms instead of offering his services exclusively virtually via the Internet.
4. They should, of course, have fulfilled all the formal requirements for opening their own practice (tax number, entry in the medical register, and membership of the Chamber of Psychotherapists and the Medical Association).
5. He should have fulfilled the necessary marketing measures (telephone number, business card, internet presence, and a publicly issued certificate of his license)

Any trained psychotherapist can easily fulfill all the criteria listed. What distinguishes a successful beginner from those who fail? All psychotherapists start by practicing their psychotherapeutic services with their relatives and friends free of charge. Their loved ones expect this help to continue free of charge for an indefinite period of time. When they open their own practice, this relationship changes. The therapist becomes legally responsible for his services. This responsibility, which the therapist bears, should have a price. This is the risk that the therapist must live with.

M. Vlajkov, *Basics of Rational-Emotive Behavior Therapy*,
https://doi.org/10.1007/978-3-032-19448-0_36

He can offer his nearest and dearest a reduced price, but he should not treat them for free, because this treatment would then be of no value to their friends. The first real patients can be recruited from this circle of friends and relatives. The friends and relatives who need therapy are the first to benefit from his expertise, and they appreciate his help. He should therefore begin his independent work with these people and tell them openly that his services come at a cost as a result of this institutionalization. The relationship between him and his first patients changes from a friendly one to a professional one. In a polite but self-confident manner, he should explain to all these people that he has practice, telephone, and marketing costs and that he has to earn his own living through this work.

The next step is to turn an open practice into a "well-run" one. As psychotherapists are only allowed to advertise their own services to a limited extent, a "newly opened" therapist should primarily acquire patients through word of mouth.

One of the most important publicity measures for beginners is to appear in public as often as possible and give talks on overcoming emotional blocks. If a therapist gets access to local mass media to publish their professional articles, they should not miss this opportunity.

Many therapists live in the false conviction that membership in elite clubs (golf club, Rotary or Lions Club, etc.) could help them. However, established doctors and therapists have long since joined these clubs, making it difficult for them to gain access, and this "field has long since been grazed." In contrast, public appearances at specialist events are highly recommended. Professionals are usually interested in recommending the services of a competent psychotherapist to their own patients, especially if they are unable to help them themselves.

A therapist who wants to set up their own practice usually has an idea of what this practice should look like and how it should be organized. In the therapist's mind, a prestigious practice consists of a reception area with a personal assistant to the therapist and a treatment room in which the therapist sits enthroned behind his desk like a king. Should a depressed or anxious patient enter such a practice, they must first overcome the "obstacle" of the assistant, who is not only interested in simply passing the patient on to the therapist, but also in presenting herself as necessary. An anxious patient will feel their fear in such situations and will probably flee the situation "headlong." A depressed patient, who has no drive, will not be able to do this.

"obstacle" as insurmountable and give up his attempt to get treatment.

The therapist should make sure that he does not ask his patient any intimate questions or express any personal curiosity during the initial contact, as this will provoke mistrust and resistance from his patient. For example, if the therapist asks a patient about his sexual preferences who has approached him because of a conflict with his boss, he is very likely to lose this patient. This question would, of course, be justified if the patient had come to solve his sexual problems.

The best advertisement for a therapist is therefore his patients. However, therapists should know that it is not enough to "just" satisfy their patients. Because "only" satisfied patients do not "bring" new patients.

Only enthusiastic patients are willing to tell others about the therapist with admiration and spread the word of mouth!

Chapter 37
The First Contact

Patients typically attend therapy at the recommendation of a third party. However, they only do so when their emotional state prevents them from coping properly with their everyday lives. The reasons they come to the practice are often anxiety or depression. Two patient groups can be distinguished. The first group consists of those who seek help on their own initiative. The second consists of those who have been pressured, coerced, or blackmailed into therapy. Depressive patients often do not register for therapy because they feel they need it (they do not believe that anyone can help them anyway), but because they have been pressured into it by their fellow human beings.

The therapist should approach patients from the two groups differently. If two patients present to the therapist at the same time, one of whom has volunteered for therapy and the other who has been pressured into treatment, the therapist should immediately admit the patient who has decided to undergo therapy on their own initiative, as they will otherwise look for another therapist, as they will not be able to overcome their suffering in the long term.

The other patient, who has been forced into therapy, can easily wait for therapy to begin because they have not come out of a state of suffering, and their motivation to actively participate in therapy will not deteriorate. If the therapist has time for the "forced" patient, he will say the following: "Now that you have appeared here once and have to spend an hour with me, I suggest that we make the best of it for you by explaining to you what my therapy consists of and how you can benefit from it."

M. Vlajkov, *Basics of Rational-Emotive Behavior Therapy*,
https://doi.org/10.1007/978-3-032-19448-0_37

Explanations About the Theoretical Framework of the Therapeutic Process

It is only at this point in the initial contact that the therapist asks their patient why they have contacted them. The answer may be that the patient came because of a personal recommendation from a third party or that they found the therapist through internet research. If the therapist accepts this answer to his question, then he cannot start the therapy because the patient has not yet named his real problem. In this case, the therapist should repeat the question but first use the patient's statement to put the patient in a good mood by praising the patient's statements.

Only after the patient has named an emotional or practical problem does the therapist begin to explain the framework of the therapy. If the patient understands that an emotional problem arises from his thinking, he has gained cognitive insight. If the therapist gives further memorable examples, the patient begins to understand that he can transfer his cognitive insights into emotional ones. If the patient indicates that he has already had several therapeutic attempts (systemic therapy, psychoanalysis, behavioral therapy, Gestalt therapy, NLP and the like), then the therapist knows that his patient has been indoctrinated with a certain therapeutic model and that his effort will be significantly greater with such patients than with those who are approaching a therapist for the first time.

For example, suppose the therapist has a psychoanalytically experienced patient and explains to them that the first step in solving their problems is to gain cognitive insight. In that case, this patient will see the therapist as a psychoanalytically oriented therapist, as everything in psychoanalysis can be traced back to the concept of "insight." The therapist should take enough time to clearly explain the difference between their therapeutic approach and the approach to which the patient has previously been exposed, which implies that the therapist should know all other approaches and be able to look at them critically.

The attention of emotionally disturbed patients is usually poor. They can only temporarily retain the information the therapist explains to them in their short-term memory. The therapist should take this fact into account and not assume that the patient will recall what has already been explained in the next session. A cognitive insight is that the patient has understood the effects of thinking on feeling. However, if he has only intellectually understood the connection between thinking and feeling, but has never experienced it emotionally, he cannot yet solve his emotional problems. Therefore, the therapist's most important task is to bring about the patient's emotional insight. Ideally, the therapist should ensure that the patient is in a pleasant mood. From this pleasant mood, the patient gains emotional insight.

Another critical aspect of the first contact with the patient is to identify the resources that have helped them to deal with their problems up to this point. The question "How have you managed to live with these blockages up to now? What have you done to overcome them?." These questions make it possible to diagnose the problems that the patient has not been able to solve with their own resources. These problems then become a central aspect of further therapy.

Patients typically report that they only felt unburdened by their unresolved problems when they distracted themselves with other activities. This fact indicates that most patients tend to distract themselves from their problems and "free" themselves from them in this way instead of confronting and solving their problems. Patients generally repress emotional problems and cope with them by distracting themselves. Just as painkillers are taken to relieve headaches, patients suffering from emotional problems use various activities (computer games, television, shopping, alcohol consumption, smoking, etc.) to distract themselves.

A reliable question to determine the patient's resources is: "What would you recommend to your friends if they had approached you with the same problem?." A patient can answer this question in three different ways:

1. "I don't know how to help them." The therapist then presents the cognitive approach and explains the ABC model, emphasizing the B–C connection.
2. "I would recommend that they do sports, go shopping or go to the movies."—The therapist then explains the difference between palliative and problem-solving methods.
3. "I would explain to them the cognitive approach and the fact that their thinking is causing their problems."—The therapist accepts this explanation and praises the patient.

Chapter 38
The Psychodiagnostics Examination

Therapists can begin therapy with a new patient in two different ways. Either they start intuitively, without having a complete picture of the clinical problems, or they conduct a thorough psychodiagnostics assessment to develop a therapeutic plan. Both approaches have certain advantages and disadvantages. The intuitive approach saves the patient time and allows the therapist to address the problem bothering the patient most immediately. This approach is only recommended for experienced therapists who can accurately diagnose the patient's underlying problem during the first session. The danger of the intuitive approach is that the therapist only addresses the problem presented by the patient. He cannot know whether it is the most critical problem or just a shame problem.

The main disadvantage of the structured approach is that a psychodiagnostics examination is very time-consuming. At the end of this examination, the patient has the impression that it has been of no use to them. This can significantly reduce their motivation to continue therapy. The advantages of the structured approach are that the therapist knows exactly how to address the patient's needs. Based on the results of this examination, he can create a precise therapy plan together with his patient and prioritize the problems.

Additionally, therapeutic progress can be measured objectively from one session to the next. The so-called "outcome questionnaire" is used for this purpose. Only after several years of therapeutic experience can a therapist confidently omit these measures and still effectively deal with patients. An experienced therapist combines the advantages of both the intuitive and the structured approach.

M. Vlajkov, *Basics of Rational-Emotive Behavior Therapy*,
https://doi.org/10.1007/978-3-032-19448-0_38

The First Trial Session

Most therapists only begin active therapy in the second session. The author recommends conducting a probationary session at the first contact with the patient. This would have the following advantages:

1. The patient gets the impression that he has already been helped in the first session.
2. If the therapist uses the first session solely for psychodiagnostics, the patient may perceive this as an incomplete session and go home dissatisfied, which would exacerbate their problems.
3. During a trial session, the therapist establishes how the patient will react to this type of therapy. In addition, the patient can get to know the therapist better during their work and decide whether they would like to continue the treatment.
4. Based on the trial session, it is possible to predict whether the therapy is likely to be successful. If the treatment is promising, the therapist motivates the patient.

A few years ago, the author had a client who, after three trial sessions, concluded that this type of therapy did not suit her. She claimed that REBT was an emotionless and mentally stressful therapy. This patient sought more support and validation of her perspective from the therapist. She also expected more empathy and a warm emotional relationship from the therapist. She also wanted the therapist to listen to her more and let her finish her own thoughts instead of limiting her rambling explanations. As the author was not prepared to fulfill these expectations, he ended the therapeutic process. For the continuation of the therapy after the completion of several probationary sessions, at least three of the following criteria should be met:

1. The relationship between the therapist and their patient is based on mutual trust.
2. The patient understands the cognitive approach.
3. The patient agrees to do his therapeutic homework regularly.
4. Both the therapist and the client realize that the therapy has already helped.
5. The patient is confident that he will be able to resolve open his emotional problems independently soon.

Chapter 39
Conclusions

1. REBT Is Highly Structured and Pragmatic

The therapy is organized around a clear, step-by-step structure (ABC Model: Activating Event, Belief, Consequence), focusing on providing therapists and clients with practical tools to resolve emotional problems both in and outside the session.

2. Emphasis on Identifying and Changing Irrational Beliefs

Unhealthy emotions mainly stem from irrational beliefs, especially absolutistic demands, catastrophizing, global ratings, and low frustration tolerance. Therapy focuses on identifying, disputing, and replacing these with rational, flexible alternatives.

3. Clear Distinction Between Healthy and Unhealthy Feelings

REBT makes a relevant distinction between healthy (functional) and unhealthy (dysfunctional) feelings, with the latter always causing suffering, cognitive blockades, and maladaptive behaviour. The goal is not to eliminate unpleasant feelings but to replace unhealthy ones with healthy—yet sometimes still unpleasant—emotions.

M. Vlajkov, *Basics of Rational-Emotive Behavior Therapy*,
https://doi.org/10.1007/978-3-032-19448-0_39

4. Therapeutic Efficiency and Client Empowerment

REBT is designed to produce rapid and sustainable results, often in fewer sessions than other psychotherapies. Clients are empowered with techniques and knowledge to maintain progress and solve future problems independently (bibliotherapy and homework assignments are key).

5. Comprehensive Error Analysis for Continual Improvement

A significant part of the manuscript is dedicated to examining therapeutic errors, emphasizing the importance of for REBT application of theory, structured procedure, and therapist self-reflection.

6. Role of Homework and Active Client Participation

Assigning and practicing homework tasks is critical to transfer insights into daily life. The therapy is active and diREBTive, requiring patient engagement during and between sessions.

7. Therapist Skills and Attitude Are Central

The effectiveness of REBT depends on the therapist's skill in applying the method, understanding of the client's problems, and maintaining a professional yet motivating therapeutic relationship.

8. Critique of Alternative Approaches

The manuscript contrasts REBT with approaches like psychoanalysis and positive thinking, arguing that diREBT engagement with irrational beliefs achieves more profound, more lasting change than less structured or solely supportive therapies.

9. Flexible, Evidence-Based Methodology

REBT integrates empirical research, philosophical roots (notably Stoicism), and learning theory, offering techniques adaptable to diverse client needs (including group and one-session treatments).

10. Ultimate Goal: Autonomous, Resilient Living

The overarching aim is to install a philosophy of increased frustration tolerance, unconditional acceptance, and cognitive resilience in clients, enabling them to face future challenges without continued therapist support.

These conclusions reflect both the theoretical foundations and practical lessons detailed throughout the manuscript, highlighting REBT's structured, efficient, and empowering approach to philosophical, emotional and behavioural change.

Chapter 40
Recommendations for Future Research

1. Empirical Validation of Structured Protocols:
   - Conduct controlled studies comparing the step-by-step, highly structured approach detailed in this manuscript to less structured REBT and other cognitive-behavioral therapies. Assess outcomes related to speed and durability of change, client empowerment, and skill retention.
   - To measure the therapy effects, construct standardized psychodiagnostics instruments (questionnaires, scales and tests).
2. Therapeutic Error Analysis:
   - Systematically investigate common therapist errors in REBT (as categorized in the manuscript: theory, diagnosis, process, relationship, etc.). Develop and validate competency checklists and training modules to reduce these errors.
3. Cultural Adaptation and Diversity:
   - Explore the cross-cultural applicability of REBT principles, especially the distinction between healthy and unhealthy emotions and the focus on disputing absolutistic demands. Qualitative research could assess how different populations interpret and integrate these concepts.
4. Homework Assignments and Self-Efficacy:
   - Examine the impact of various types of homework assignments (cognitive, emotive, behavioral, complex) on treatment adherence, skill generalization, and relapse prevention. Investigate digital or app-based delivery to increase engagement.

M. Vlajkov, *Basics of Rational-Emotive Behavior Therapy*,
https://doi.org/10.1007/978-3-032-19448-0_40

Table 40.1 Recommendations and research

Domain	Recommendation
Research	Controlled studies, error analysis, cultural work
Practice	Standardized training, therapeutic skill building incl. humor
Supervision	Error-based feedback, outcome monitoring
Public Health	Patient materials (handouts, booklets, workbooks, stickers), self-help bibliotherapy, education (workshops, seminars)

5. One-Session Treatment and Brief Interventions:

   - Further test the efficacy and boundaries of "one-session treatment" for specific phobias and other conditions. Comparative studies with standard multi-session approaches would clarify indications and long-term outcomes.

6. Supervision and Therapist Development:

   - Develop models for ongoing supervision tailored to the pragmatic, error-focused REBT approach. Research should examine outcomes for therapists (e.g., error reduction, self-efficacy, and burnout prevention).

Recommendations for Clinical and Professional Practice

1. Standardization of REBT Training:

   - Integrate the step-by-step process outlined in the manuscript into curricula for therapists and supervisors, emphasizing error minimization, skill acquisition, and active client collaboration.

2. Therapeutic Relationship as a Tool, Not Goal:

   - Continue educating practitioners on using the therapeutic relationship to foster engagement and insight—while maintaining the focus on skill transfer and independence, not dependency.

3. Use of Humor and Flexible Methods:

   - Encourage therapists to develop and refine the use of humor and storytelling in therapy as described in the book for strengthening insight, resilience, and client-therapist rapport.

4. Client Empowerment and Termination:

   - Train therapists to actively promote client autonomy by using bibliotherapy and explicit skill transfer, and to normalize and coach healthy termination as a positive goal.

5. Outcome Measurement and Feedback:

   - Routinely collect outcome and satisfaction data using tools inspired by the manuscript (e.g., outcome questionnaires, checklists for structured session steps). Use this for continuous quality improvement.

6. Bibliotherapy and Public Engagement:
   - Develop patient-facing materials (handouts, workbooks, apps) using the structured methods and language of the manuscript. Encourage public education efforts that demystify REBT and highlight its self-help potential.

This systematic approach will strengthen REBT's evidence base, broaden its reach, and further empower both practitioners and clients.

Appendices

Appendix 1

Transcript of a therapeutic session with the author's comments (in italics)
This transcription is based on a true story. The patient's data is anonymized. If anyone recognizes themselves in parts of the transcript, this is only due to chance.

Therapist (T): I would first like to explain to you what we are going to do today. Please answer my questions as precisely and concretely as possible. Neither you nor I is interested in excessive descriptions and explanations. We both know that you are in a convalescent phase after a major surgical procedure. We also know that you are suffering from significant emotional disturbances, but we don't yet know exactly which ones. Possible disorders include anxiety, stress, uncertainty, insecurity, depression, despair, apathy, fits of rage, feelings of guilt, and the like. Please tell me how you feel about the cancer you have had removed. What are you suffering from, and what is bothering you the most at the moment?

The therapist has begun the therapeutic process with introductory facts that help build a trusting relationship. In the last part of this introduction, the therapist focused his patient's attention on the most critical problem, aiming to provide him with additional motivation and the prospect that it could be solved.

Patient (P): What worries me most is my future. Will I be able to livelike I used to?

T: What kind of feeling is that? Do you just feel worried oranxious?

The therapist uses this question to determine whether the problem is a clinically relevant one (fear of the future).

P: Both!

M. Vlajkov, *Basics of Rational-Emotive Behavior Therapy*, https://doi.org/10.1007/978-3-032-19448-0

The therapist uses this opportunity to clarify the difference between clinically relevant and other emotional problems.

T: In your situation, worrying is a healthy feeling, and feelingAnxiety is worse than just being anxious. That's why anxiety isan unhealthy feeling. Humans have the ability to feel all emotions.Feelings can be both pleasant and unpleasant. Pleasant feelingsare okay! Most people feel pleasant when they are incircumstances that suit them. However, if something badhappens, people start to feel unpleasant. Unpleasant feelings canbe both healthy and unhealthy. Whether a feeling in a situation isunhealthy can be recognized by the following signs:

- The person is mentally blocked, their own thinking goes round in circles, and they can't find a way out of these musings. They ask themselves: "What should I do? How can I help myself?"
- The person suffers and feels psychological pain.
- The person usually experiences acute physical symptoms, such as muscle cramps, sweating, palpitations, and leg weakness.
- The person behaves inappropriately in the situation. Either they flee or they try to change the situation by force. This results in either aggressive or self-destructive behavior.
- In the long term, the person may begin to suffer from psychosomatic problems: Allergies, immune deficiencies, chronic headaches, digestive disorders, high blood pressure, hormonal disorders, neurovegetative disorders, etc.

In one and the same negative situation, some people only feel anxious, and this feeling is healthy, while others feel anxious. This anxiety is unhealthy and inhibiting. A healthy, uncomfortable feeling means that the person

- is not mentally blocked and can think clearly.
- She is not suffering; she feels insecure and worried,
- And she has no acute physical symptoms but is in an optimal condition for the situation.
- Behaves corREBTly and faultlessly and
- does not suffer from any psychosomatic disorders, but their health improves and is promoted.

The therapist used the didactic method in this part of the therapy because he knew that the patient would receive an audio recording of this session.

T: So, you can feel unpleasantly healthy or unpleasantlyunhealthy in the same situation. What do you think it dependson how you will feel?

This was the first attempt to draw the patient's attention to the B-C connection.

P: From my attitude. I should choose the path I take for myself.

T: You mean your way of thinking. Your attitude, the way youthink about the situation.

P: Yes, from the way I think.

T: So, since you feel the fear, when and in which situations dothis fear become stronger? Please tell me about a specific situationin which you have felt this fear!

P: When I'm about to have another medical examination, I getscared as hell.

T: What are you afraid of in this situation?

P: Before I get the wrong diagnosis again, like last time.

T: Let's assume that the doctors make the wrong diagnosis again.What would that mean for you?

This is where the therapist starts an inference chaining process.

P: That may trigger something in me again – wait, what did youask me?

T: Let's assume they get the wrong diagnosis again.
What would that mean for you?

P: Then that would be bad for me again. But how can I knowwhether the diagnosis is wrong or right?

T: So,youthinkthedoctorsshouldmakeacorREBTdiagnosisforyouthistime?

P: Of course.

The core thought pattern of fear was identified.

T: And if you think that the doctors should give you a corREBT diagnosis, how will you feel?

The B-C connection was confirmed using the specific example of the patient.

P: Desperate and anxious.

T: As long as you think that the doctors have to give you a corREBTdiagnosis without you being able to control them, you will feelanxiety.

P: That's right.

This is the confirmation of the B-C connection and the precise formulation of the irrational belief. Now the dispute begins, with which this irrational belief is checked.

T: Why would the doctors have to make a corREBT diagnosis for you?

P: Because they claim that their method is 100 percent successful.Doctors advise every patient to undergo such an examination.

T: A week ago in the meeting, you stated that the probability ofa corREBT diagnosis is 97 percent. The probability of an incorREBTdiagnosis is therefore three percent. Is that corREBT?

P: Absolutely.

T: So, when you go for an examination, the result can either bea wrong or a corREBT diagnosis. Can the percentage valuesexpress this, or is it an "either-or – decision?

P: Either-or.

T: From this, we can both conclude that the probability calculationdoes not work in individual cases. My question to you again:Do the doctors have to make a corREBT diagnosis for you underall circumstances, or would this only be desirable?

P: Of course, I expect the doctors to make a 100 percent corREBTdiagnosis, although I know that this would only be desirable.

T: Is there a guarantee that doctors will never give you an incorREBTdiagnosis?

P: No, there is no such guarantee.

T: So, your absolutistic demand that the doctors don't give you thewrong diagnosis be implemented?

P: That's right, it doesn't depend on me.

T: Do you want the doctors to give you a corREBT diagnosis? Doesthis wish would have the power to force the doctors to fulfill yourwish?In other words, is it logical to think that just because you havea wish, it must therefore be fulfilled?

P: It's not like that in life, but in life situations like this …

T: … do you mean critical situations in which a mistake is possibleand even probable, it should not happen under any circumstances?

P: Only where a mistake could have fatal consequences.

T: How have you fared so far? Have your doctors already madeone or more fatal mistakes in your treatment or diagnosis?

P: Unfortunately, they have.

T: What can we expect from the next diagnosis or treatment?

P: You know what? If you've ever experienced an accident like this,it must never happen to you again!

T: And what about the probability?

P: The probability always exists.

T: What's better for you then?

P: I accept this probability.

T: Now I would like to suggest a new way of thinking. It is asfollows: It would be nice if doctors made all diagnoses with onehundred percent certainty, but since this is not possible, they don'thave to.

The therapist formulates the rational alternative here.

P: Yes, that's not an imperative.

T: If you formulate reality as it is, how do you feel? Pleasecompare your feelings when you accept the possibility of errorwith the statement that the doctors must make a corREBTdiagnosis for me under all circumstances! Think about itimmediately afterwards: It would be nice if the diagnosis were corREBT, which it probably will be, but there is no guarantee ofthat! How do you feel in this case?

P: I can't be happy with it, but I can come to terms with it.

T: And once you've come to terms with it, how does that makeyou feel?

P: Now I have found my inner peace. I'm not afraid of the nextmedical examination.

T: Are you worried? Are you probably not happy about havingto undergo another examination?

P: I'm not happy about it, but I don't feel anxious anymore.

The therapist begins to examine the second irrational belief.

T: Is it terrible that your doctors keep making one mistake oranother with you?

P: It was cruel that I was wrongly diagnosed. But now, two monthsafter the wrong diagnosis, I'm feeling better again, and althoughI'm facing chemotherapy and radiotherapy, I'm taking it all in mystride.

T: In this session, we first established what was bothering you themost. That was your inhibiting fear. We then discovered whenthis fear comes up for you. This happens when you anticipate theupcoming examination. Finally, we identified the thought thatcauses this anxiety – that the results of the medical examinationmust be 100 percent reliable. We then examined this idea, andtogether we concluded that there is no guarantee andthat the results do not have to be reliable, even though you would likethem to be.

With this summary, the therapist has concluded the therapeutic process and now expects his patient to reformulate his own thinking.

T: Please tell us in your own words what your new way ofthinking is?

P: It would be nice if the doctors would not make any incorREBTdiagnoses with me in the future, but as there is no guarantee ofthis, they are allowed to make mistakes with me too.

T: Would that be a disaster for you or just a majorinconvenience?

P: It would be very unpleasant, but not a disaster. It was only adisaster the first time, and when I look at it now, with a bit ofdistance, I know that it wasn't a real disaster, just a biginconvenience.

T: Since you experienced this experience as a catastrophe at thetime, and what happened then has not changed in the meantime,except that you no longer feel so anxious about it, it is clear thatyour assessment of the situation at the time was the cause ofyour feeling of catastrophe.

With this statement, the therapist reinforces his patient's rational alternative. Finally, the therapist gives the corresponding therapeutic homework. In the further course of the therapy, the therapist strives for an even deeper therapeutic change in the patient. This consists of the patient developing a preferential way of thinking about their reality. This is referred to as the patient's new philosophy of life.

Appendix 2

Table A1 Example of a table for checking irrational beliefs

C – Unhealthy feeling	B – irrational belief	D – Dispute (Examination of the irrational belief and formulation of the rational alternative)
Anger at the driver who cut in while he was driving	He wasn't allowed to do that, the idiot!	Is it right to think that just because I don't want to be "cut" that it won't happen? Can I undo the fact that I was "cut" while driving? Obviously, this kind of thing happens all the time in road traffic. This is probably proof that People are allowed to break the law! The rational belief is that although I don't want other drivers to "cut" me, it happens and will probably happen again and again in the future, which just goes to show that they are allowed to do it because they decide for themselves whether to do it. And I have no way of stopping them!

Bibliography

American Psychiatric Association. (1994). *Diagnostic and statistical manual of mental disorders* (4th ed.). American Psychiatric Association.

American Psychiatric Association. (2013). *Diagnostic and statistical manual of mental disorders* (5th ed.). American Psychiatric Association.

Beck, A. T. (1979). *Cognitive therapy and the emotional disorders.* International Universities Press.

Beck, J. S. (1995). *Cognitive behavior therapy: Basics and beyond.* Guilford Press.

Cialdini, R. B. (2018). *Influence: The psychology of persuasion* (Rev. ed.). Harper Business.

Clark, D. A., & Beck, A. T. (2011). *Cognitive therapy of anxiety disorders: Science and practice* (Updated ed.). Guilford Press.

Dryden, W. (1995). *Rational emotive behavior therapy: A reader.* Sage Publications.

Ellis, A., & Harper, R. A. (1975). *A new guide to rational living*. Prentice-Hall.

Ellis, A. (1957). *How to live with a neurotic.* Crown Publishers.

Ellis, A. (1977). *Anger: How to live with and without it.* Citadel Press.

Ellis, A. (1994). *Reason and emotion in psychotherapy.* Citadel Press.

Ellis, A. (1996). *Better, deeper, and more enduring brief therapy.* Institute for Rational-Emotive Therapy.

Ellis, A. (2001). *Overcoming destructive beliefs, feelings, and behaviors: New diREBTions for rational emotive behavior therapy*. Prometheus Books.

Ellis, A. (2002). *Overcoming resistance: A rational emotive behavior therapy integrated approach.* Springer Publishing.

Ellis, A. (2004). *Rational emotive behavior therapy: It works for me – it can work for you.* Prometheus Books.

Ellis, A. (2005). *The road to tolerance: The philosophy of rational emotive behavior therapy.* Prometheus Books.

Ellis, A. (2019). How to stop destroying your relationship: A guide to enjoyable dating, mating, and relating (Posthumous ed.). Robinson.

Ellis, A., & Dryden, W. (1997). *The practice of rational emotive behavior therapy.* Springer Publishing.

Ellis, A., & Abrams, M. (2009). *Personality theories: Critical perspectives* (2nd ed.). Sage Publications.

Ellis, A., & MacLaren, C. (1998). *Rational emotive behavior therapy: A therapist's guide*. Impact Publishers.

Ellis, A., & Tafrate, R. C. (1998). *How to control your anger before it controls you.* Citadel Press.

M. Vlajkov, *Basics of Rational-Emotive Behavior Therapy*, https://doi.org/10.1007/978-3-032-19448-0

Gillespie, R. (1991). **Manufacturing knowledge: A history of the Hawthorne experiments*. Cambridge University Press.
Gilovich, T., & Ross, L. (2023). *The wisest one in the room: How you can benefit from social psychology's most powerful insights* (2nd ed.). Free Press.
Korzybski, A. (1933). *Science and sanity: An introduction to non-Aristotelian systems and general semantics*. Institute of General Semantics.
Maultsby, M. C., Jr. (1990). *You and your emotions*. Rational Self-Help Books.
Maultsby, M. C., Jr. (1990). *Rational behavior therapy*. Seaton Foundation.
Nielsen, S. L., Johnson, W. B., & Ellis, A. (2001). *Counseling and psychotherapy with religious persons: A rational emotive behavior therapy approach*. Lawrence Erlbaum Associates.
Öst (2014). Specific phobias. In D. H. Barlow (Ed.), *Clinical handbook of psychological disorders: A step-by-step treatment manual.* Guilford Press.
Öst, L.-G., Davis, T. E., III, & Ollendick, T. H. (Eds.). (2012). *Intensive one-session treatment of specific phobias*. Springer.
Peseschkian, N. (1985). *In search of meaning: A psychotherapy of small steps*. Springer-Verlag.
Peseschkian, N. (2016). *Positive psychotherapy of everyday life: A self-help guide for individuals, couples and families with 250 case stories.* AuthorHouse UK.
Peseschkian, N. (2016). *Positive psychosomatics: Clinical manual of positive psychotherapy.* AuthorHouse.
Seligman, M. E. P. (1975). *Helplessness: On depression, development, and death.* W. H. Freeman.
Seligman, M. E. P. (1990). *Learned optimism: How to change your mind and your life.* Knopf.
Seligman, M. E. P. (2004). *Authentic happiness: Using the new positive psychology to realize your potential for lasting fulfillment*. Free Press.
Vlajkov, M. (2000). *The ATOS method: The psychology of balance*. Kognitives Management Verlag.
Walen, S. R., DiGiuseppe, R., & Dryden, W. (1992). *A practitioner's guide to rational-emotive therapy.* Oxford University Press.
Wessler, R. A., & Wessler, R. L. (1980). *The principles and practice of rational-emotive therapy.* Jossey-Bass.
World Health Organization. (1992). *The ICD-10 classification of mental and behavioural disorders: Clinical descriptions and diagnostic guidelines.* World Health Organization.
World Health Organization. (2019). *International statistical classification of diseases and related health problems* (11th rev.; ICD-11). https://icd.who.int/
Xian, J. (2009). *How do you tame an elephant and a monkey?*Wern er Kristkeitz *Verlag*.
Young, J. E., Klosko, J. S., & Weishaar, M. E. (2005). *Schema therapy: A practitioner's guide.* Guilford Press.

Index

M. Vlajkov, *Basics of Rational-Emotive Behavior Therapy*, https://doi.org/10.1007/978-3-032-19448-0

MIX
Papier aus verantwortungsvollen Quellen
Paper from responsible sources
FSC® C105338

If you have any concerns about our products,
you can contact us on
ProductSafety@springernature.com

In case Publisher is established outside the EU,
the EU authorized representative is:
Springer Nature Customer Service Center GmbH
Europaplatz 3, 69115 Heidelberg, Germany

Printed by Libri Plureos GmbH
in Hamburg, Germany